BLACK & DECKER

HOME IMPROVEMENT LIBRARY™

Building Decks

CREATIVE
PUBLISHING
international

MINNETONKA, MINNESOTA

Contents

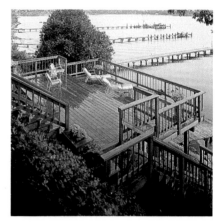

Introduction **5**
Deck Styles 6

Building Decks **43**

Building Decks: A Step-
  by-Step Overview 44
Installing a Ledger 46
Locating Post Footings . 52
Digging & Pouring
  Footings 58
Setting Posts 62

Installing a Beam 68
Hanging Joists 72
Laying Decking 79
Building Stairs 82
Installing a Deck
  Railing 88

Feature Decks **97**

Platform Deck 99
Diamond-pattern
  Deck 105

Island Deck 110

Copyright © 1991
Creative Publishing international, Inc.
5900 Green Oak Drive
Minnetonka, Minnesota 55343
1-800-328-3895
All rights reserved
Printed in U.S.A.

Books available in this series:
*Everyday Home Repairs, Decorating With
Paint & Wallcovering, Carpentry: Tools •
Shelves • Walls • Doors, Building Decks,
Kitchen Remodeling, Home Plumbing Projects
& Repairs, Basic Wiring & Electrical Repairs,
Workshop Tips & Techniques, Advanced
Home Wiring, Carpentry: Remodeling,
Landscape Design & Construction,
Bathroom Remodeling, Built-in Projects for
the Home, Kitchen & Bathroom Ideas,
Refinishing & Finishing Wood, Exterior
Home Repairs & Improvements, Home
Masonry Repairs & Projects, Building
Porches & Patios, Deck & Landscape Ideas,
Flooring Projects & Techniques, Advanced
Deck Building, Advanced Home Plumbing*

Library of Congress
Cataloging-in-Publication Data

Building decks.

p. cm.--(Black & Decker home improvement
library)
Includes index.
ISBN 0-86573-708-8 (hardcover).
ISBN 0-86573-709-6 (softcover).
1. Decks (Architecture, Domestic)
Design and construction
I. Cy DeCosse Incorporated. II. Series.
TH4970.B85 1990
690'.184--dc20   89-23708

President: Iain Macfarlane

Created by: The Editors of Creative
Publishing international, Inc., in cooperation
with Black & Decker. ● **BLACK&DECKER** is a
trademark of the Black & Decker
Corporation and is used under license.

Deck Basics 13

Parts of a Deck 14
Decking Patterns 16
Stairways 18
Railings 19
Lumber Basics 20
Pressure-treated
    Lumber 22

Redwood & Cedar 23
Lumber Size & Deck
    Planning 24
Hardware &
    Fasteners 26
Concrete 28
Tool Basics 31

Design & Planning 33

Creating Site Drawings . 34
Drawing Design
    Plans 36

Ordering Lumber
    & Materials 40

Index 126

Deck Finishing & Repair 117

Finishing a New Deck . 118
Maintaining a Deck . . . 120

Repairing a Deck 122

Project Director: John Riha
Senior Art Director: Tim Himsel
Editor: Bryan Trandem
Technical Production Editor: Paul Currie
Project Manager: Dianne Talmage
Art Directors: Dave Schelitzche, Brad
  Springer
Copy Editors: Janice Cauley, Bernice
  Maehren
Production Manager: Jim Bindas
Assistant Production Managers: Julie
  Churchill, Amelia Merz
Shop Director: Greg Wallace
Set Builders: John Hasselbalch, Larry
  Kolegue, Brad Spleiss

Production Staff: Sheila DiPaola, Joe Fahey,
  Kevin D. Frakes, Yelena Konrardy, Scott
  Lamoureux, Daniel Meyers, Linda
  Schloegel, Nik Wogstad
Director of Photography: Tony Kubat
Studio Manager: Cathleen Shannon
Assistant Studio Manager: Rebecca DaWald
Photographers: Paul Englund, Rex Irmen,
  John Lauenstein, Mark Macemon, Mette
  Nielsen
Contributing Photography: Lea Babcock; Milt
  Charno & Associates, Inc.; George Lyons
Models: Kari Shoutz, Douglas Snyder

Contributing Editor: Jim Hufnagel
Contributing Manufacturers: American
  Brush Company, Inc.; California Redwood
  Association; Cooper Industries; Hickson
  Corporation; The Irwin Company; Kop-
  Coat, Inc.; P & M Cedar Products, Inc.;
  Quality Wood Treating Co.; United Steel
  Products Co.; Western Wood Products
  Association

Printed on American paper by:
  R.R. Donnelley & Sons Co.
10 9 8 7 6 5 4

Introduction

Building a deck is one of the most popular do-it-yourself projects. A deck adds value to a home and creates additional living space for sunning, entertaining, or enjoying warm weather. With a few carpentry skills and a basic knowledge of tools, any homeowner can construct a durable and beautiful deck.

Building Decks is designed to give you the skills and knowledge necessary to plan, build, and finish your deck. Hundreds of close-up, color photographs illustrate every detail of the building process and guarantee your success.

This introduction is followed by six pages of photographs that show completed decks. Each deck is unique, and offers ideas for the size, shape, and location of your project.

After this selection of deck ideas, a chapter on Deck Basics teaches you the tools, fasteners, materials, and terminology necessary for deck construction. Learn why stairs, railings and decking patterns influence how your deck is built.

With this basic knowledge, you are ready to design your deck. The next chapter, Design & Planning, includes step-by-step instructions on how to draw site plans, and how to use those plans to create a finished deck design. Finally, use your deck design to estimate the lumber and materials needed for the job.

The third chapter, Building Decks, is one of the most complete manuals of deck construction ever published. More than 175 color photographs show each step of building a deck, from installing the ledger and laying out footings to putting the final touches on the deck railing. This attention to detail ensures your success.

Next, watch three different full-scale decks being constructed before your eyes. We've divided each project into eight distinct stages and given you a grandstand view of the process. You'll gain a thorough understanding of construction and see how decking styles determine framing patterns.

A final section, Deck Finishing & Repair, shows you how to care for your deck, protect it from the elements, and keep it beautiful. In addition, we show you how to repair an older deck so that you can enjoy it for many years to come.

We are pleased to present *Building Decks*, and know you will find this fine book to be an excellent addition to your Home Improvement Library.

NOTICE TO READERS

This book provides useful instructions, but we cannot anticipate all of your working conditions or the characteristics of your materials and tools. For safety, you should use caution, care and good judgment when following the procedures described in this book. Consider your own skill level and the instructions and safety precautions associated with the various tools and materials shown. Neither the publisher nor Black & Decker® can assume responsibility for any damage to property or injury to persons as a result of misuse of the information provided.

The instructions in the book conform to "The Uniform Plumbing Code," "The National Electrical Code Reference Book," and "The Uniform Building Code" current at the time of its original publication. Consult your local Building Department for information on building permits, codes and other laws as they apply to your project.

Photo by Blakesee-Lane, courtesy P & M Cedar Products, Inc.

Deck Styles

A deck is an extension of your living space. It allows you to enjoy fresh air and the out-of-doors in comfort and safety. Built correctly, a deck is strong, weatherproof, and will last for many years.

Plan your deck with your house site and the surrounding landscaping in mind. There are many factors to consider in planning the shape, size, and location of a deck. Some features will be more important to you than others. Keep these features in mind as you design and build your deck.

Study the photographs on the next few pages to see how other homeowners planned and built according to their unique circumstances.

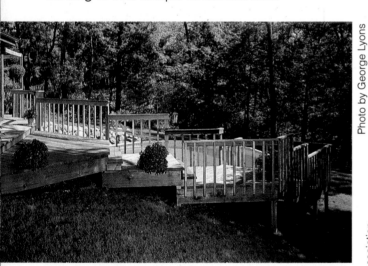

This multilevel deck (above) follows the contour of the land. It takes advantage of slopes that otherwise would get little use.

Viewing areas (right) are important considerations in this deck plan. It offers an open and unrestricted line of sight for scenic views.

Photo by George Lyons

California Redwood Association

A single-level deck is easy to build. A door leading to the kitchen allows easy access for entertaining or barbecuing. Added features include benches and an overhead trellis that offers relief from midday sun.

Photo by George Lyons

Use trees as design elements. This midwestern deck is built around several oak trees. Rather than restrict the design or remove the trees, the homeowner framed openings for the trees.

Photo by George Lyons

Entertainment areas are highlighted with this well-designed deck that includes a built-in fire pit, a hot tub, a porch swing, and sunset views to the west.

California Redwood Association

Warm climate deck allows year-round use. This California deck includes a large roofed area for shelter during rainy weather, and a cabinet for convenient food preparation.

California Redwood Association

A sun-filled deck with platform stairs has a wide, unobstructed surface. This deck was designed around nearby landscaping. The backyard arrangement gives an unrestricted view of the rural countryside.

Photo by George Lyons

A platform deck is ideal for a flat, level lot. It is easy to construct and, because of the low height, does not require railings. This deck features built-in planter boxes, benches, and access to a three-season porch.

Photo by George Lyons

Create visual interest in a small deck with planter boxes, an overhead arbor, and changes in levels. A variety of decking patterns adds texture.

Photo by George Lyons

Add privacy with a lattice fence and well-planned landscaping. This deck takes advantage of surrounding trees and shrubs.

Photo by George Lyons

Multiuse decks (above and right) are designed with a variety of needs in mind. They include areas for dining, sunning, conversation, and access to pool areas. Different levels help define each area.

This freestanding deck (below) uses platform design and ceramic tile accents. Its features include a food preparation area, hot tub, privacy fence, and built-in lighting, benches, and planter boxes.

Deck Basics

Parts of a Deck

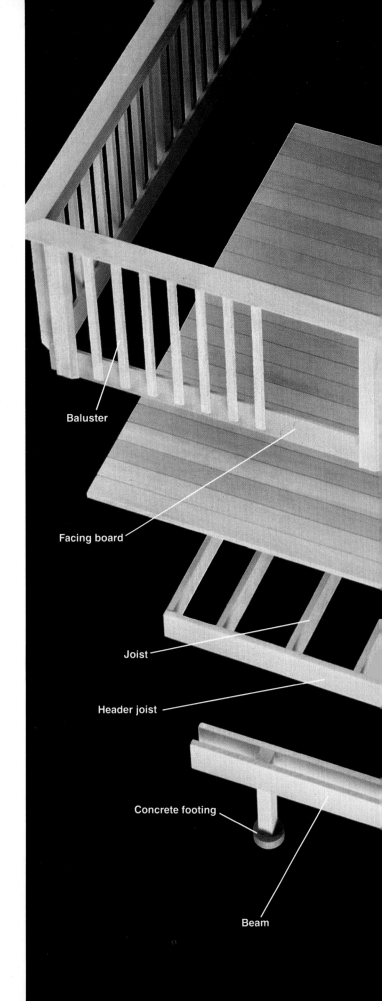

Baluster

Facing board

Joist

Header joist

Concrete footing

Beam

Structural parts of a deck include posts, beams, ledgers, and joists. They support and distribute the weight of the deck. For economy and durability, use pressure-treated lumber for these parts. The other parts of a deck include the decking, facing, railings, and stairway. Use redwood or cedar for these visible parts.

Ledgers anchor an attached deck to a house. Ledgers support one end of all joists.

Concrete footings with post anchors support the weight of the deck and hold the deck posts in place. They are made by pouring concrete into tube forms. Local climates and building codes determine depth of footings. **Post anchors** should be made of galvanized steel to resist corrosion.

Posts transfer the weight of the deck to the footings. They are attached to the post anchors with galvanized nails, and to the beam with lag screws.

Beams provide the main structural support for the deck. A beam is usually made from a pair of 2×8s or 2×10s attached to the deck posts.

Joists support the decking. For an attached deck, the joists are fastened at one end to the **ledger**, and at the other end to the **header joist**. The **outside joists** can be covered with redwood or cedar **facing** boards for appearance.

Decking is the main feature of any deck. The decking boards are attached to the joists with galvanized screws or nails.

Railing parts include **railing posts** and **balusters** attached to the header and outside joists, a horizontal **rail,** and a **cap**. Building codes may require railings on decks 24" or more above ground level.

A stairway is made from a pair of **stringers** fastened to the side of the deck, and a series of **treads** attached to the stringers with metal cleats.

Cap

Rail

Decking

Railing post

Joist hanger

Ledger

Baluster

Tread

Stringer

Stairway post

Outside joist

Deck post

Post anchor

Decking Patterns

Decking is an important element of a deck, and can be installed using a variety of board sizes and design patterns. The decking pattern determines the spacing and layout of the joists. For example, a normal, straight decking pattern requires joists that are spaced 16" on-center. A diagonal decking

Diagonal pattern adds visual interest to a deck. Diagonal patterns require joists that are spaced closer together than for straight patterns.

Parquet pattern requires double joists and blocking to provide a supporting surface for attaching the butted ends of decking boards.

pattern requires that the joist spacing be 12" on-center. Parquet patterns and some other designs may require extra support, like double joists or extra blocking. For sturdy, flat decking, use 2 × 4 or 2 × 6 lumber. Thinner lumber is more likely to twist or cup.

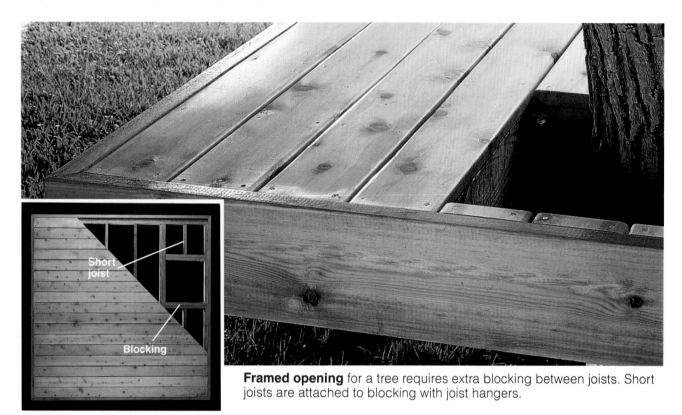

Framed opening for a tree requires extra blocking between joists. Short joists are attached to blocking with joist hangers.

Border pattern gives an elegant, finished look to a deck. Install trim joists to support the border decking.

Stairways

A stairway provides access to a deck from the yard or patio. Its position also helps establish traffic patterns across the deck.

Build the stairway with lumber that matches the rest of the deck. If possible, stair treads should use the same board pattern as the surface decking. On decks more than 24" high, local codes may require stairway handrails.

Platform steps feature wide treads. Each step is built on a framework of posts and joists.

Stairway Styles

Open steps have metal cleats that hold the treads between the stringers. The treads on this stairway are built with 2 × 6s to match the surface decking.

Boxed steps, built with notched stringers and solid risers, give a finished look to a deck stairway. Predrill ends of treads to prevent splitting.

Long stairways sometimes require landings. A landing is a small platform to which both flights of stairs are attached.

Railings

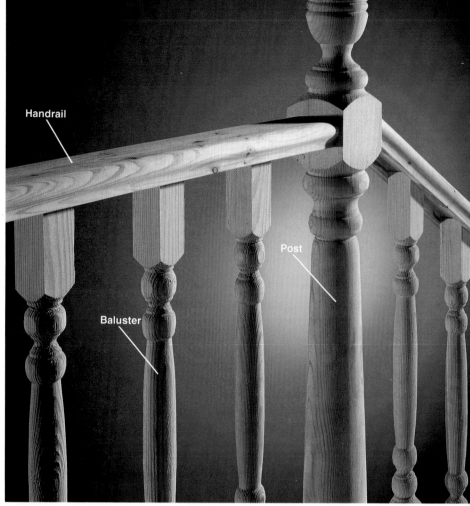

Railings usually are required by building code on any deck that is more than 24" high. Select a railing design that fits the style of your home.

For example, on a low, ranch-style house, choose a deck railing with wide, horizontal rails. On a Tudor-style home with a steep roof, choose a railing with closely spaced, vertical balusters.

Preshaped products let you easily build decorative deck railings. Railing products include shaped handrails, balusters, and posts.

Railing Styles

Vertical balusters with posts and rails are a good choice for houses with strong vertical lines. A vertical baluster railing like the one shown above is a good choice where children will be present.

Horizontal railings are often used on low, ranch-style homes. Horizontal railing is made of vertical posts, two or more wide horizontal rails, and a railing cap.

Lattice panels add a decorative touch to a deck. They also provide extra privacy.

Lumber Basics

Lumber used to construct a deck must be resistant to rot and insect damage. The three types of wood recommended for deck construction are: heartwood grade redwood, heartwood cedar, and pressure-treated lumber.

The reddish heartwoods of both redwood and cedar have natural decay resistance. The sapwood of redwood and cedar is lighter in color than the heartwood and has less resistance to decay. Sapwood must be treated with a clear sealer-preservative if used outdoors.

Pressure-treated lumber is treated with chemical preservatives. The preservative most often used for decking lumber is chromated copper arsenate, identified by the label "CCA."

Inspect each piece of lumber, and return any pieces that are severely warped or cracked. Avoid any boards that have large knots, especially where strength is essential, like joists or stairways.

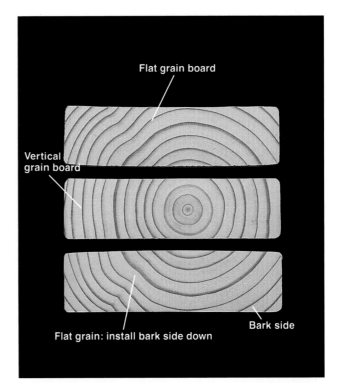

Inspect lumber for flaws. Sight along each board to check for warping and twisting. Return any boards with serious flaws. Check for large or loose knots. Boards used for structural parts should be knot-free (clear), or should have only small knots that are tight and ingrown.

Check end grain of decking boards. Boards with flat grain tend to "cup," and can trap standing water if not installed properly. Recent research indicates that flat grain boards cup toward the bark side (not away from it, as was previously thought in the industry), and should be installed so the bark side faces down.

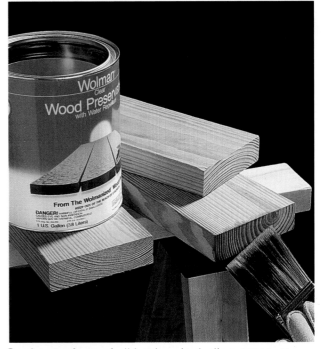

Store lumber so that it stays dry and warp-free. Use supports to keep the wood stack a few inches off the ground. Use spacer blocks to support each row of lumber, and to allow air circulation between boards. Cover the lumber stack with heavy plastic or a water-proof tarp.

Seal cut edges of all lumber, including pressure-treated wood, by brushing on clear liquid sealer-preservative. Chemicals used in pressure treatment do not always penetrate completely. Sealer-preservative protects all types of wood from rot.

Pressure-treated Lumber

Pressure-treated lumber is the strongest and least expensive choice for deck lumber. Pressure-treated lumber resists rot and insects and is an excellent building material for outdoor use.

Treated lumber is created by forcing chemical preservatives into it under high pressure. The most common treatment uses chromated copper arsenate, identified by the label "CCA." The preservative usually gives the wood a green color, which fades with time. Or, you can stain pressure-treated wood in a variety of colors.

Pressure-treated lumber is rated by the amount of chemical retained by the wood. For decks, choose lumber with a retention level of .40, approved for direct ground contact. This is sometimes signified by the code "LP 22" stamped on the wood.

Pressure-treated lumber can be used to build the entire deck; or, it can be used only for posts, beams, and joists, with redwood or cedar used for decking, stairways, facing, and railings.

Caution:
The chemicals in pressure-treated lumber are toxic. Wear eye protection, a particle mask, and long sleeves and pants to avoid contact with sawdust from pressure-treated wood.

Grade stamp for pressure-treated lumber lists the type of preservative used and the chemical retention level of the wood. Look for "CCA" label indicating that chromated copper arsenate is the preservative. Make sure lumber carries the label "LP 22," or ".40 retention." Other information found on grade stamp includes proper exposure rating, and name and location of treating company.

Redwood

Redwood is an attractive wood often used for outdoor structures. The heartwood has a brownish red color and is naturally resistant to decay. The cream-colored sapwood should be treated with wood preservative when used in a deck.

Quality redwood is somewhat expensive, so it is often used only for visible parts of the deck, like decking and railings.

Redwood is available in more than 30 grades. "Construction heart" or "merchantable heart" are medium-quality grades that are good choices for a deck.

Cedar

The cedar species recommended for decks include red cedar and incense cedar. Cedar has a light brown appearance, with an attractive grain. Because it ages to a uniform silver-gray, cedar is often used where a weathered appearance is desired.

Heartwood cedar is naturally resistant to decay. Sapwood cedar is white or cream-colored, and should be treated with wood preservative when used in a deck.

Cedar can be used for the visible surfaces of the deck. For structural members like joists, beams, and posts, use pressure-treated lumber.

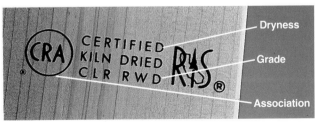

Grade stamp for redwood lists wood dryness, lumber grade, and membership association. Redwood should be certified "KILN DRIED" or "DRY"; and graded as clear redwood (CLR RWD), construction heartwood (CONST HT), merchantable heartwood (MERCH HT), or construction redwood (CONST RWD).

Grade stamp for cedar lists the lumber mill number, the moisture content, the species, the lumber grade, and membership association. Western red cedar (WRC) or incense cedar (INC) used in decks should be graded as heartwood (HEART) with a maximum moisture content of 15% (MC 15).

Lumber Size & Deck Planning

A deck has seven major structural parts: the **ledger, decking, joists,** one or more **beams, posts, stairway stringers,** and **stairway treads.** To create a working design plan, you must know the span limits of each part of the deck. The ledger is attached directly to the house and does not have a span limit.

A span limit is the safe distance a board can cross without support from underneath. The maximum safe span depends on the size of the board. For example, 2 × 6 joists spaced 16" on-center can safely span 9' 9", while 2 × 10 joists can span 16' 5".

Begin planning by first choosing size and pattern of the decking. Then determine the size and layout of the joists, beams, and posts, using the span tables on the opposite page. In general, a deck designed with larger-size lumber, like 2 × 12 joists and beams, requires fewer pieces, because the boards have a large span limit.

Nominal	Actual
1 × 4	¾" × 3¾"
1 × 6	¾" × 5¾"
2 × 4	1½" × 3½"
2 × 6	1½" × 5½"
2 × 8	1½" × 7¼"
2 × 10	1½" × 9¼"
2 × 12	1½" × 11¼"
4 × 4	3½" × 3½"
6 × 6	5½" × 5½"

Nominal vs. Actual Lumber Dimensions: When planning a deck, remember that the actual size of lumber is smaller than the nominal size by which lumber is sold. Use the actual dimensions when drawing a deck design plan.

Recommended Decking Span Between Joists:
Decking boards can be made from a variety of lumber sizes. For a basic deck use 2 × 4 or 2 × 6 lumber with joists spaced 16" apart.

Decking Boards	Recommended Span
1 × 4 or 1 × 6, laid straight	16"
1 × 4 or 1 × 6, laid diagonal	12"
2 × 4 or 2 × 6, laid straight	16"
2 × 4 or 2 × 6, laid diagonal	12"
2 × 4, laid on edge	24"

Maximum Joist Span Between Supports: Maximum joist span between supports depends on the size of the joists and the spacing between joists. For example, a deck with 2 × 8 joists spaced 16" apart requires supports no more than 12' 10" apart. On a cantilevered deck, the joists may extend past the beam by a distance equal to one-third the total length of the joists.

Joist Size	Joist Spacing (on center)		
	12"	16"	24"
2 × 6	11' 7"	9' 9"	7' 11"
2 × 8	15' 0"	12' 10"	10' 6"
2 × 10	19' 6"	16' 5"	13' 4"

Maximum Beam Span Between Posts: Maximum beam span depends on the size of the beams and their spacing. For example, a deck with a 4 × 8 beam, and joists that span 12 feet should have posts that are no more than 7 feet apart.

Beam Size	Joist Span			
	6 ft.	8 ft.	10 ft.	12 ft.
4 × 6 (two 2 × 6s)	8 ft.	7 ft.	6 ft.	5 ft.
4 × 8 (two 2 × 8s)	10 ft.	9 ft.	8 ft.	7 ft.
4 × 10 (two 2 × 10s)	12 ft.	11 ft.	10 ft.	9 ft.
4 × 12 (two 2 × 12s)	14 ft.	13 ft.	12 ft.	11 ft.

Recommended Post Size: Choose post size by finding the load area for the deck. To find the load area, multiply the distance between beams by the distance between posts. For example, on a deck that has one beam spaced 10 feet from the ledger, with posts spaced 7 feet apart, the load area is 70. If this deck is less than 6 feet high, the recommended post size is 4 × 4.

	Load Area Multiply distance between beams (feet) times the distance between posts (feet).				
Deck Height	48	72	96	120	144
Up to 6 ft.	4 × 4	4 × 4	6 × 6	6 × 6	6 × 6
More than 6 ft.	6 × 6	6 × 6	6 × 6	6 × 6	6 × 6

Minimum Stair Stringer Sizes: Size of stair stringers depends on the span of the stairway. For example, if the bottom of the stairway lies 7 feet from the deck, build the stringers from 2 × 12s.

Span of Stairway	Stringer Size
Up to 6 ft.	2 × 10
More than 6 ft.	2 × 12

Recommended Railing Sizes: Size of posts, rails, and caps depends on the spacing of the railing posts. For example, if railing posts are spaced 6 feet apart, use 4 × 4 posts and 2 × 6 rails and caps.

Space Between Railing Posts	Post Size	Cap Size	Rail Size
2 ft. to 3 ft.	2 × 4	2 × 4	2 × 4
3 ft. to 4 ft.	4 × 4	2 × 4	2 × 4
4 ft. to 6 ft.	4 × 4	2 × 6	2 × 6

6" J-bolt with washer and nut

1¼" joist nail

10d nail

2½" deck screw

8d nail

¼" × 1¼" lag screw

⅜" × 4" lag screw

1" washer

1" washer

⅜" × 5" lag screw

Hardware & Fasteners

Build your deck with galvanized lumber connectors, nails, and screws. Galvanized metal products resist rust and will not stain the wood.

Metal lumber connectors are used to create strong joints with wood framing members. Post anchors, joist hangers, and brackets are available at lumberyards and home improvement centers.

Seal heads of counterbored screws with silicone caulk to prevent water damage.

Hot-dipped galvanized nails (above) have a thick zinc coating and rough surface. Hot-dipped nails will not rust or stain wood.

Deck fasteners (left), include 6" J-bolt with nut and washer, 8d and 10d galvanized nails, 1¼" galvanized joist nail, 2½" corrosion-resistant deck screw, ¼" × 1¼" lag screw, ⅜" × 4" lag screw, ⅜" × 5" lag screw, and 1" washer.

Flashing fits over ledger to protect wood from moisture damage. Top edge of flashing tucks up under the siding.

Masonry anchors with lag screws hold the ledger to stone, brick, or concrete blocks.

J-bolts with nuts and washers hold the post anchors to the concrete footings.

Post anchors hold deck posts in place, and raise the base of the posts to help prevent water from entering end grain of wood.

Angle brackets help reinforce header and outside joists. Angle brackets are also used to attach stair stringers to the deck.

Joist hangers are used to attach joists to the ledger and header joist. Double hanger is used when decking pattern requires a double-width joist.

Angled joist hangers are used to frame decks that have unusual angles or decking patterns.

Stair cleats support the treads of deck steps. Cleats are attached to stair stringers with 1/4" × 1 1/4" galvanized lag screws.

Silicone caulk seals lag screw heads and any cracks that may trap water. Choose an exterior-grade caulk rated for lifetime use.

Concrete

Use concrete to make solid footings that will support the weight of the deck. Concrete for footings is made from a mixture of portland cement, sand, and coarse gravel (¼" to 1½" in diameter). These materials can be purchased separately and mixed at home, or you can buy bags containing the pre-mixed dry ingredients. For larger amounts, buy ready-mixed concrete in trailer loads.

For most deck projects, mixing your own concrete is easy and inexpensive. Mix concrete in a wheelbarrow or with a power mixer, available at tool rental centers.

The estimation charts on the opposite page give approximate volumes of concrete. You may have a small amount of concrete left over after pouring post footings.

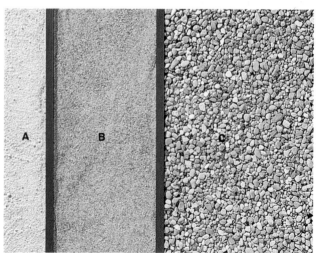

Mix concrete ingredients in a wheelbarrow. Use a ratio of 1 part portland cement (A), 2 parts sand (B), and 3 parts coarse gravel (C). Or, use the cubic-foot volumes shown in the chart (page opposite).

Amount of Concrete Needed (cubic feet)

Number of 8" Diameter Footings	Depth of Footings (feet)			
	1	2	3	4
2	¾	1½	2¼	3
3	1	2¼	3½	4½
4	1½	3	4½	6
5	2	3¾	5¾	7½

Concrete Ingredient Amounts

Amount of Concrete Needed (cubic feet)	Dry Ingredients for Self-mix			60-lb. bags of premixed dry concrete
	94-lb. bags of portland cement	Cubic feet of sand	Cubic feet of gravel	
1	⅙	⅓	½	2
2	⅓	⅔	1	4
3	½	1½	3	6
4	¾	1¾	3½	8
5	1	2¼	4½	10
10	2	4½	9	20

Buying & Mixing Concrete

Buy premixed bags of dry concrete for small jobs. A 60-lb. bag creates about ½ of a cubic foot of concrete. A 90-lb. bag creates about ⅔ of a cubic foot.

Rent a power cement mixer to blend large amounts of cement, gravel, sand, and water quickly.

Buy ready-mixed concrete for larger jobs. Trailer loads are available at rental centers, and are sold by the cubic yard. One cubic yard equals 27 cubic feet.

Ratchet wrench & socket

Shovel

Trowel

Metal snips

22-oz. claw hammer

32-oz. masonry hammer

Cat's paw

Hoe

50-ft. tape measure

16-ft. tape measure

Caulk gun

Rubber mallet

Clamshell posthole digger

Combination square

Mason's string

Compass

Plumb bob

Flat pry bar

Line level

Scratch awl

Torpedo level

Chalk line

1" chisel

Putty knife

Level

Framing square

Hand tools for deck building should have heavy-duty construction. Metal tools should be made from high-carbon steel with smoothly finished surfaces. Buy quality hand tools that are well balanced, and that have tight, comfortably molded handles. There is no substitute for quality.

Tool Basics

With a set of basic hand and power tools, you can complete any of the deck projects shown in this book. You may already own many of the tools needed. If you buy new tools, invest in quality, heavy-duty products that will provide long service.

Some specialty tools, like power miter boxes or reciprocating saws, are available at tool rental centers. Or, they can be purchased at home improvement stores.

Always wear eye protection when using tools. Always wear a particle mask and work gloves when sawing or handling pressure-treated lumber, because the chemicals in the wood are toxic.

Tools for finishing and maintaining a deck include: . rubber gloves (A), shop vacuum (B), 14-gauge extension cord (C), pressure sprayer (D), hydraulic jack and handle (E), eye protection (F), scrub brush (G), paint brush (H), particle mask (I), and orbital sander (J).

Power tools include: power miter box (A), circular saw (B) with carbide-tipped blade and Teflon®-coated carbide blade, reciprocating saw (C), ⅜'' drill and bits (D), jig saw (E), and screwgun (F). These tools should have heavy-duty motors. Screwgun is designed for driving long deck screws through 2'' lumber. Reciprocating saw and power miter box can be purchased at home centers, or leased at tool rental outlets.

Design & Planning

Make a map of the features of your house and yard. Include any features that might affect how you build and use your deck, like sun and shade patterns, trees, and other landscaping details. For accurate measurements, use a long tape measure and hold it level and perpendicular to the house.

Creating Site Drawings

Create site drawings of the building area before designing a deck. Show all details that may affect how you build and use the deck.

Building a deck requires two types of site drawings. A **plan view** shows the building site as viewed from directly overhead. An **elevation** shows the vertical details of the site as it is viewed from the side or front.

As you create site drawings, consider how the features of house and yard influence the deck design. Remember that the building site is affected by weather, time of day, and seasonal changes.

For example, if your deck will be used mainly for summertime evening meals, look at the sun, shade, and wind patterns on the site during this time of day.

Everything You Need:

Tools: pencil or marker, eraser, 50-ft. tape measure, ruler, compass, line level.

Materials: large sheets of paper.

Supplies: mason's string.

How to Create Plan-view Site Drawings

1 Sketch position of house and yard on a large sheet of paper, using a scale of 1" equals 1 foot. Show position of doors, windows, and outdoor utilities, like garden hose spigots, or light fixtures.

2 Add a symbol to the site drawing to indicate north. Mark the location of trees, gardening beds or planters, and any other landscaping features. Show any overhead or underground utility lines.

3 Observe the deck site during the time of day when the deck will be used most often. Outline shade and sun patterns on the site drawing.

4 Show how the site changes throughout the day. Outline shade and sun patterns at different times, and quality of nearby view. Note changes in winds, traffic noise, and neighborhood activity.

How to Create Elevation Site Drawings

1 Create a side-view elevation map of your site, showing the slope of the ground and the position of the house. For accuracy, stretch level mason's strings from the house, and use the strings for reference to determine slope of ground.

2 Add any other features that will affect how you build and use the deck, like the height of tree branches or telephone wires, shrubs, flowerbeds, or other landscaping details.

Drawing Design Plans

Design plans help you estimate lumber and hardware needs, and provide the measurements needed to lay out the deck and cut the lumber. If a work permit is required by local codes, you must have design plans.

You will need two types of design drawings for a deck project. A **plan view** shows the parts of the deck as they are viewed from directly overhead. An **elevation** shows the deck parts as viewed from the side or front.

To avoid confusion, do not try to show all parts of the deck in a single plan view. First, draw one plan that shows the outline of the deck and the pattern of the decking boards. Then make another plan that shows the underlying ledger, joists, beams, and posts.

Everything You Need:

Tools: pencil or marker, eraser, ruler.

Materials: site drawing, large sheets of paper, sheets of tissue paper.

How to Draw Design Plans

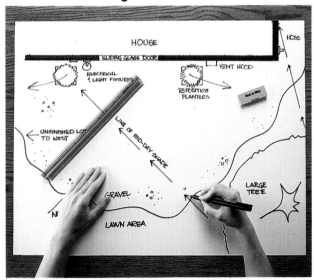

1 Use the scaled site drawings (pages 34 to 35) to help establish the size and shape of the deck.

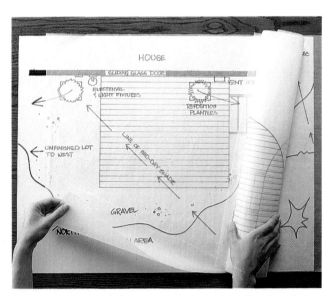

2 Lay a sheet of tissue paper over the site drawing and tape in position. Experiment with deck ideas by sketching different designs on separate sheets of tissue paper.

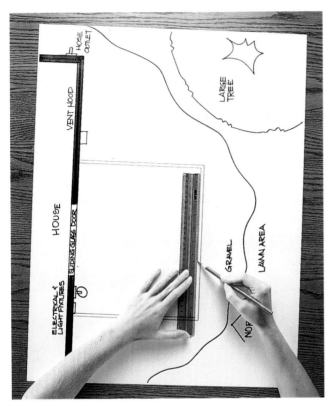

3 Make copies of the scaled site drawing. Use a ruler and sharp pencil to draw the outline of the deck on one copy of the scaled site drawing.

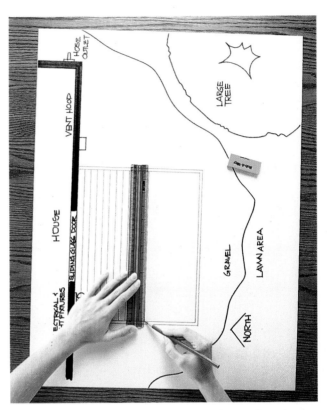

4 Draw in the decking pattern over the outline. Indicate the size and type of lumber and hardware to be used. Save this plan for reference.

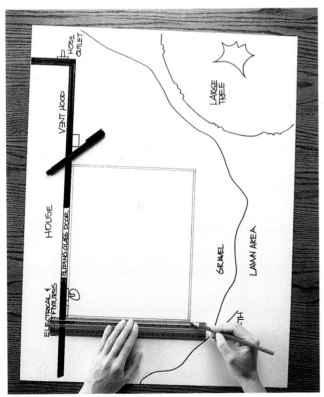

5 On a second copy of the scaled site drawing, draw another outline of the deck. Draw in the ledger, the outside joists, and the header joist.

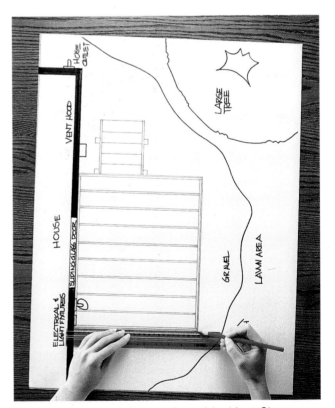

6 Draw the inner joists, and any blocking. Show any facing boards that will be used. Show the stairway stringers, treads, and posts.

(continued next page)

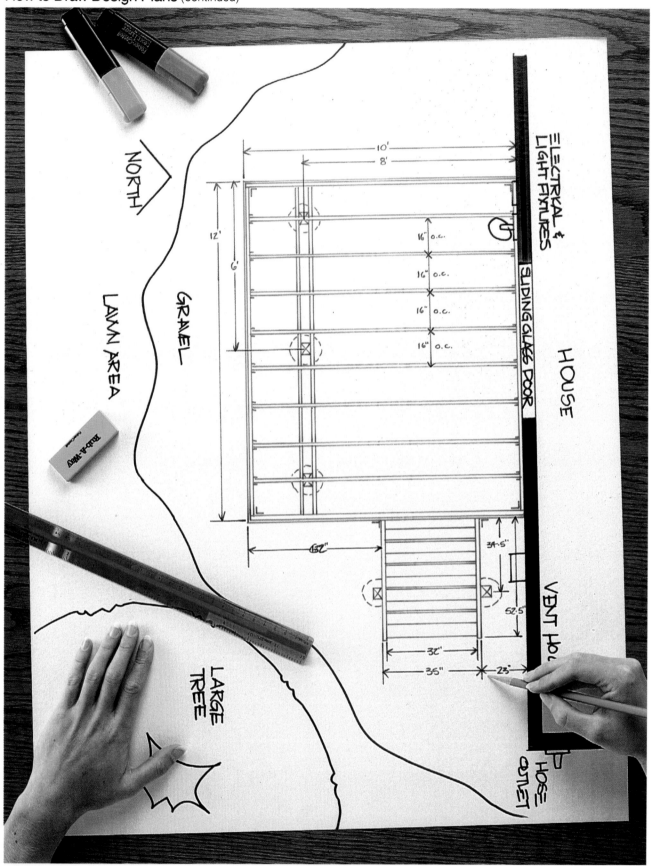

7 Draw in the deck beam and posts, and show the location of the concrete footings. List all deck dimensions on the plan. Save this drawing for reference when ordering lumber and hardware.

How to Draw Design Elevations

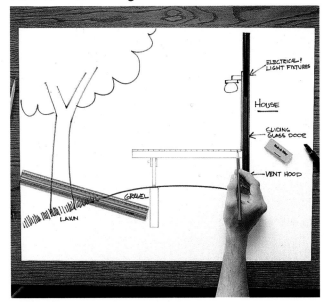

1 Draw in the basic deck platform on the site elevation drawing (page 35). Draw in the beam and the posts.

2 Add the stairway to the elevation drawing, then draw in the railing posts, balusters, rails and caps. List all dimensions on the drawing, and indicate size, type, and quantities of lumber and hardware needed. Save this drawing for reference.

3 Create another design elevation showing the deck as viewed from the front. Include all deck dimensions, and indicate the size and type of lumber and hardware to be used. Save this drawing for reference.

Ordering Lumber & Materials

Use the deck design plans and elevations to help make a complete list of the items you will need. For convenience, copy the checklist on the opposite page. Add 10% to lumber and material estimates to compensate for flaws in materials and construction errors.

Most supplies for building a deck are available at lumberyards or home improvement centers. Full-service lumberyards have a complete selection of building materials, but prices may be higher than those at home improvement centers. The quality of lumber at home centers can vary, so inspect the wood and hand-pick the pieces you want.

Order top-quality hardware, caulks, wood sealers, and stains. Save money on nails, screws, and other hardware by buying them in large quantities.

Buy top-quality products for a long-lasting deck, including: alkyd-based sealers and stains (A, B, C), galvanized post anchors (D), galvanized nails (E), galvanized joist hangers (F), corrosion-resistant deck screws (G), silicone caulk (H).

Lumber & Materials Checklist

Item	Size, type	Quantity	Where to buy	Price each	Total price
Lumber					
Ledger					
Posts					
Beams					
Joists					
Decking					
Stair stringers					
Stair treads					
Railing posts					
Balusters or rails					
Hardware					
Flashing					
Galvanized nails					
1¼" joist nails					
Post anchors					
Lag screws					
Deck screws					
Joist hangers					
Joist angle brackets					
Metal stair cleats					
Concrete					
Concrete forms					
Portland cement					
Sand					
Gravel					
Miscellaneous					
Silicone caulk					
Sealer/stain					
Equipment rental					
Tools to buy					

Photocopy this checklist for reference when ordering lumber and materials.

Building Decks

Building Decks: A Step-by-Step Overview

Review the design plan (pages 36 to 39) and the directions on pages 46 to 95 before beginning deck construction. Build the deck in several stages, and gather tools and materials for each stage before beginning. Arrange to have a helper for the more difficult stages.

Check with local utilities for the location of underground electrical, telephone, or water lines. Apply for a building permit, where required, and make sure a building inspector has approved the deck design before beginning work.

The time it takes to build a deck depends on the size and complexity of the design. A rectangular deck, about 10 ft. × 14 ft., can be completed in two or three weekends.

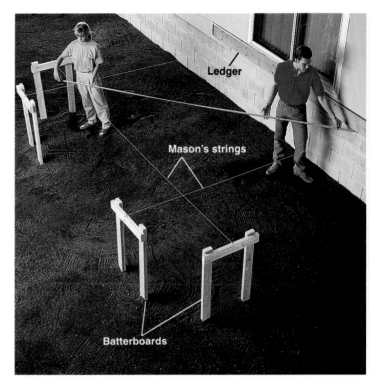

1 Install a ledger to anchor the deck to the house and to serve as reference for laying out footings (pages 46 to 51). Use batterboards and mason's strings to locate footings, and check for square by measuring diagonals (pages 52 to 57).

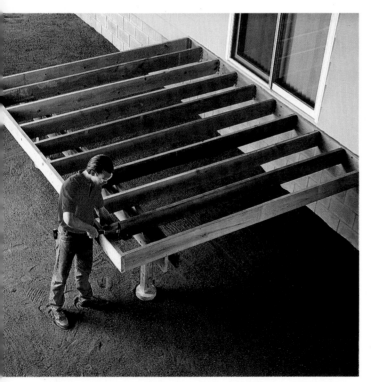

4 Install metal joist hangers on the ledger and header joist, then hang the remaining joists (pages 74 to 77). Most decking patterns require joists that are spaced 16" on center.

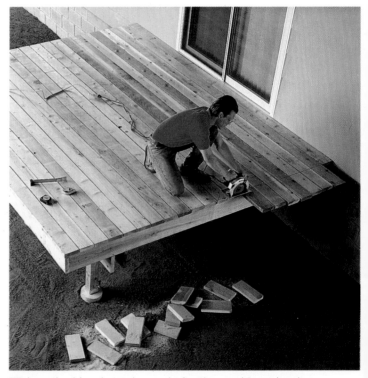

5 Lay decking boards, and trim them with a circular saw (pages 78 to 81). If desired for appearance, cover pressure-treated header and outside joists with redwood or cedar facing boards (page 81).

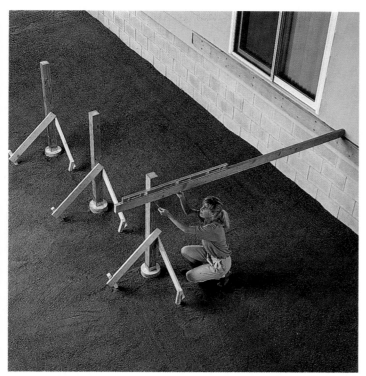

2 Pour concrete post footings (pages 58 to 61), and install metal post anchors (pages 63 to 64). Set and brace the posts, attach them to the post anchors, and mark posts to show where beam will be attached (pages 64 to 67).

3 Attach the beam to the posts (pages 68 to 71). Install the outside joists and header joist, using galvanized nails (pages 72 to 73).

Beam

Outside joists

Header joist

6 Build deck stairs (pages 82 to 87). Stairs provide access to the deck and establish traffic patterns.

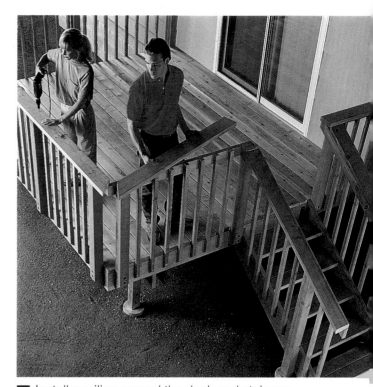

7 Install a railing around the deck and stairway (pages 88 to 95). A railing adds a decorative touch, and may be required on any deck that is more than 24" above the ground.

Installing a Ledger

The first step in building an attached deck is to fasten the ledger to the house. The ledger anchors the deck and establishes a reference point for building the deck square and level. The ledger also supports one end of all the deck joists, so it must be attached securely to the framing members of the house.

Install the ledger so that the surface of the decking boards will be 1" below the indoor floor level. This height difference prevents rainwater or melted snow from seeping into the house.

Everything You Need:

Tools (page 30): pencil, level, circular saw with carbide blade, chisel, hammer, metal snips, caulk gun, drill and bits (¼" twist, 1" spade, ⅜" and ⅝" masonry), ratchet wrench, awl, rubber mallet.

Materials: pressure-treated lumber, galvanized flashing, 8d galvanized common nails, silicone caulk, ⅜" × 4" lag screws and 1" washers, lead masonry anchors for ⅜" lag screws (for brick walls).

Supplies: 2 × 4s for braces.

Ledger (shown in cross section) is made from pressure-treated lumber. Lap siding is cut away to expose sheathing and to provide a flat surface for attaching the ledger. Galvanized flashing tucked under siding prevents moisture damage to wood. Countersunk ⅜" × 4" lag screws hold ledger to header joist inside house.

How to Attach a Ledger to Lap Siding

1 Draw an outline showing where the deck will fit against the house, using a level as a guide. Include the thickness of the outside joists and any decorative facing boards that will be installed.

2 Cut out siding along outline, using a circular saw. Set blade depth to same thickness as siding, so that blade does not cut into sheathing.

3 Use a chisel to finish the cutout where circular saw blade does not reach. Hold the chisel with the bevel-side in.

4 Measure and cut ledger from pressure-treated lumber. Remember that ledger will be shorter than overall length of cutout.

(continued next page)

5 Cut galvanized flashing to length of cutout, using metal snips. Slide flashing up under siding.

6 Center the ledger in the cutout, underneath the flashing. Brace in position, and tack ledger into place with 8d galvanized nails. Apply a thick bead of silicone caulk to crack between siding and flashing.

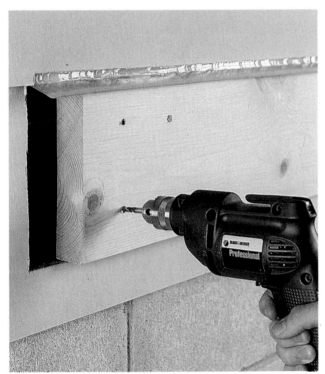

7 Drill pairs of ¼" pilot holes spaced every 2 feet, through the ledger and sheathing and into the header joist.

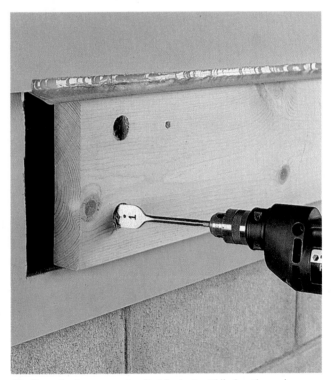

8 Counterbore each pilot hole to ½" depth, using a 1" spade bit.

9 Attach ledger to wall with ⅜" × 4" lag screws and washers, using a ratchet wrench.

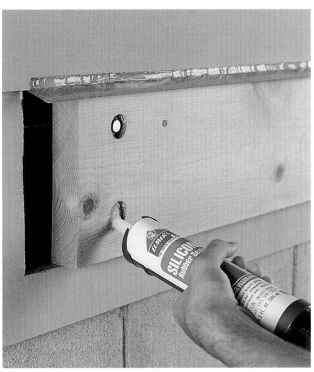

10 Seal lag screw heads with silicone caulk. Seal the crack between the wall and the sides and bottom of the ledger.

How to Attach a Ledger to Masonry

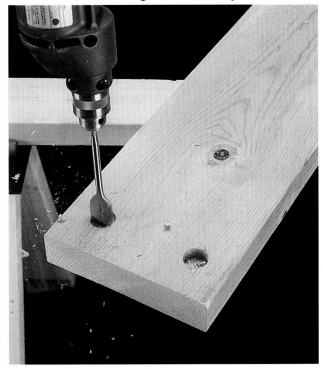

1 Measure and cut ledger. Ledger will be shorter than overall length of cutout. Drill pairs of ¼" pilot holes every 2 feet in ledger. Counterbore each pilot hole to ½" depth, using a 1" spade bit.

2 Draw an outline of the deck on the wall, using a level as a guide. Center ledger in outline on wall, and brace in position. Mark the pilot hole locations on wall, using an awl or nail. Remove ledger.

(continued next page)

3 Drill anchor holes 3" deep into masonry, using a ⅝" masonry bit.

4 Drive lead masonry anchors for ⅜" lag screws into drilled holes, using a rubber mallet.

5 Attach ledger to wall with ⅜" × 4" lag screws and washers, using a ratchet wrench. Tighten screws firmly, but do not overtighten.

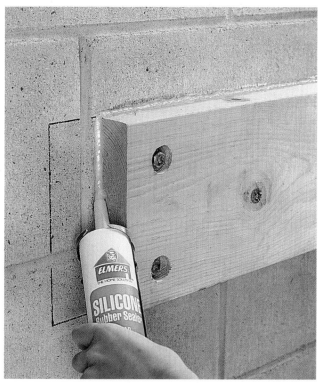

6 Seal the cracks between the wall and ledger with silicone caulk. Also seal the lag screw heads.

How to Attach a Ledger to Stucco

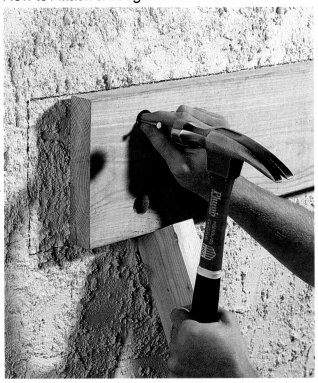

1 Draw outline of deck on wall, using a level as a guide. Measure and cut ledger, and drill pilot holes (page 49, step 1). Brace ledger against wall, and mark hole locations, using a nail or awl.

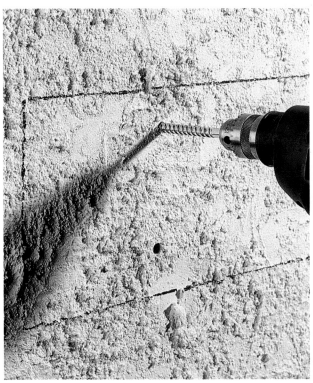

2 Remove ledger. Drill pilot holes through stucco layer of wall, using a ⅜" masonry bit.

3 Extend each pilot hole through the sheathing and into the header joist, using a ¼" bit. Reposition ledger and brace in place.

4 Attach ledger to wall with ⅜" × 4" lag screws and washers, using a ratchet wrench. Seal the lag screw heads and the cracks between the wall and ledger with silicone caulk.

Labels on image: Ledger, Plumb bob, Mason's strings, Batterboards

Mason's strings stretched between ledger and batterboards are used to position footings for deck posts. Use a plumb bob and stakes to mark the ground at the exact centerpoints of footings.

Locating Post Footings

Establish the exact locations of all concrete footings by stretching mason's strings across the site. Use the ledger board as a starting point. These perpendicular layout strings will be used to locate holes for concrete footings, and to position metal post anchors on the finished footings. Anchor the layout strings with temporary 2 × 4 supports, often called batterboards.

Everything You Need:

Tools: tape measure, felt-tipped pen, circular saw, screwgun, framing square, masonry hammer, claw hammer, line level, plumb bob.

Supplies: 2 × 4s, 10d nails, 2½" wallboard screws, mason's strings, masking tape.

How to Locate Post Footings

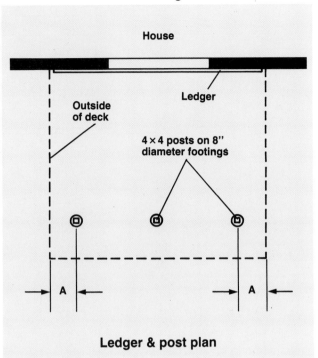

House

Ledger

Outside of deck

4 × 4 posts on 8" diameter footings

A ← → A

Ledger & post plan

1 Use the design plan (page 38) to find distance (A). Measure from the side of the deck to the center of each outside post. Use the elevation drawings (page 39) to find the height of each deck post.

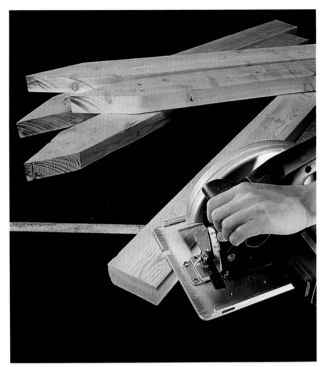

2 Cut 2 × 4 stakes for batterboards, each about 8" longer than post height. Trim one end of each stake to a point, using a circular saw. Cut 2 × 4 crosspieces, each about 2 feet long.

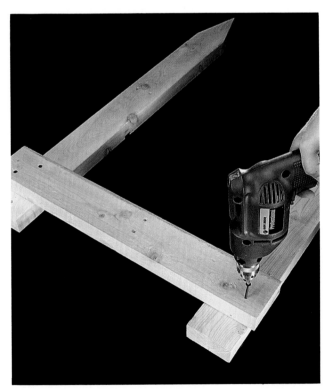

3 Assemble batterboards by attaching crosspieces to stakes with 2½" wallboard screws. Crosspieces should be about 2" below tops of stakes.

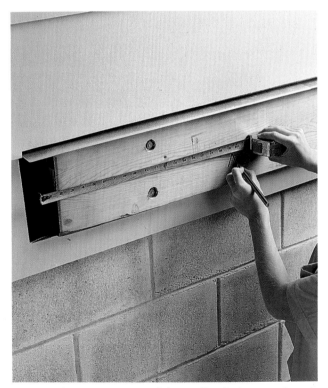

4 Transfer measurement A (step 1) to ledger, and mark reference points at each end of ledger. String lines will be stretched from these points on ledger. When measuring, remember to allow for outside joists and facing that will be butted to the ends of the ledger.

(continued next page)

5 Drive a batterboard 6" into the ground, about 2 feet past the post location. Crosspiece of batterboard should be parallel to the ledger.

6 Drive a 10d nail into bottom of ledger at reference point (step 4). Attach a mason's string to nail.

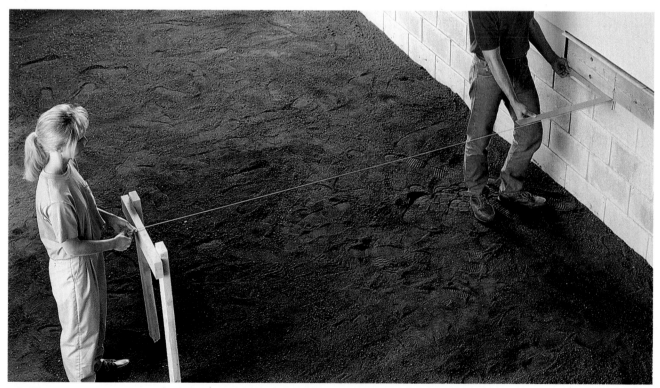

7 Extend the mason's string so that it is taut and perpendicular to the ledger. Use a framing square as a guide. Secure the string temporarily by wrapping it several times around the batterboard.

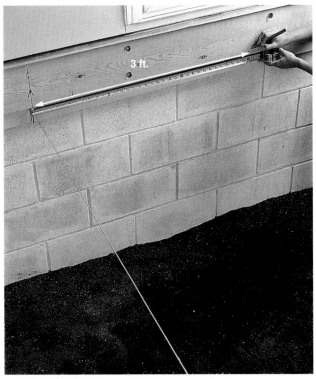

8 Check the mason's string for square using "3-4-5 carpenter's triangle." First, measure along the ledger 3 feet from the mason's string and mark a point, using a felt-tipped pen.

9 Measure mason's string 4 feet from edge of ledger, and mark with masking tape.

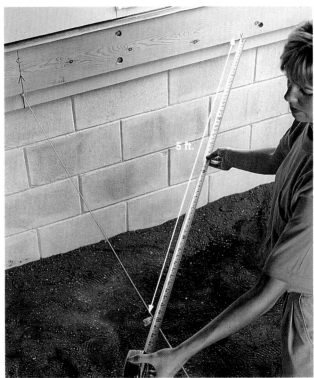

10 Measure distance between marks. If string is perpendicular to ledger, the distance will be exactly 5 feet. If necessary, move string left or right on batterboard until distance between marks is 5 feet.

11 Drive a 10d nail into top of batterboard at string location. Leave about 2" of nail exposed. Tie string to nail.

(continued next page)

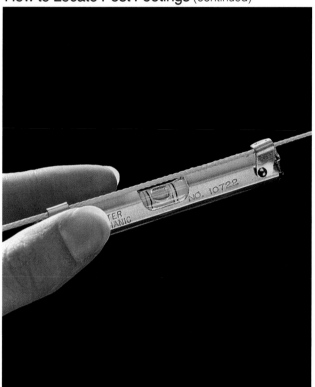

12 Hang a line level on the mason's string. Raise or lower string until it is level. Locate other outside post footing, repeating steps 5 to 12.

13 Measure along mason's strings from ledger to find centerpoint of posts. Mark centerpoints on strings, using masking tape.

14 Drive additional batterboards into ground, about 2 feet outside mason's strings and lined up with post centerpoint marks (step 13).

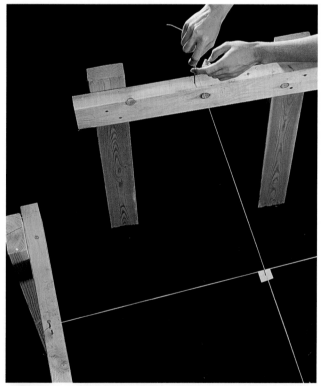

15 Align a third cross string with the centerpoint marks on the first strings. Drive 10d nails in new batterboards, and tie off cross string on nails. Cross string should be close to, but not touching, the first strings.

Cross string

16 Check strings for square by measuring distances A-B and C-D. Measure diagonals A-D and B-C from edge of ledger to opposite corners. If strings are square, measurement A-B will be same as C-D, and diagonal A-D will be same as B-C. If necessary, adjust strings on batterboards until square.

17 Measure along the cross string and mark center-points of any posts that will be installed between the outside posts.

18 Use a plumb bob to mark post centerpoints on the ground, directly under the marks on the mason's strings. Drive a stake into ground at each point. Remove mason's strings before digging footings.

Digging & Pouring Footings

Power augers quickly dig holes for post footings. They are available at rental centers. Some models can be operated by one person, while others require two people.

Concrete footings hold deck posts in place and support the weight of the deck. Check local codes to determine the size and depth of footings required for your area. In cold climates, footings must be deeper than the soil frost line.

To help protect posts from water damage, each footing should be poured so that it is 2" above ground level. Tube-shaped forms let you extend the footings above ground level.

It is easy and inexpensive to mix your own concrete by combining portland cement, sand, gravel, and water. See pages 28 to 29 for more information on buying and mixing concrete.

Before digging, consult local utilities for location of any underground electrical, telephone, or water lines that might interfere with footings.

Everything You Need:

Tools (page 30): power auger or clamshell posthole digger, tape measure, pruning saw, shovel, reciprocating saw or handsaw, torpedo level, hoe, trowel, shovel, old toothbrush, plumb bob, utility knife.

Materials: 8" concrete tube forms, portland cement, sand, gravel, J-bolts.

Supplies: wheelbarrow, scrap 2 × 4.

How to Dig & Pour Post Footings

1 Dig holes for post footings with a clamshell digger or power auger, centering the holes on the layout stakes. For holes deeper than 35", use a power auger to dig post-hole footings.

2 Measure hole depth. Local building codes specify depth of footings. Cut away tree roots, if necessary, using a pruning saw.

3 Pour 2" to 3" of loose gravel in the bottom of each footing hole. Gravel will provide drainage under concrete footings.

4 Add 2" to hole depth so that footings will be above ground level. Cut concrete tube forms to length, using a reciprocating saw or handsaw. Make sure cut is straight.

5 Insert tubes into footing holes, leaving about 2" of tube above ground level. Use a level to make sure tops of tubes are level. Pack soil around tubes to hold them in place.

(continued next page)

6 Mix dry ingredients for concrete in a wheelbarrow, using a hoe.

7 Form a hollow in center of dry concrete mixture. Slowly pour a small amount of water into hollow, and blend in dry mixture with a hoe.

8 Add more water gradually, mixing thoroughly until concrete is firm enough to hold its shape when sliced with a trowel.

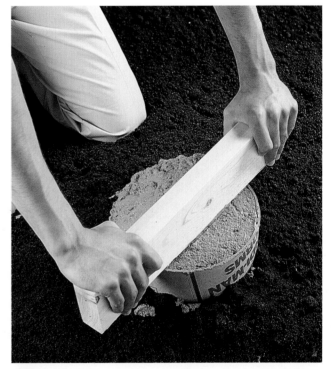

9 Pour concrete slowly into tube form, guiding concrete from wheelbarrow with a shovel. Use a long stick to tamp the concrete, filling any air gaps in the footing.

10 Level the concrete by pulling a 2 × 4 across the top of the tube form, using a sawing motion. Add concrete to any low spots. Retie the mason's strings on the batterboards, and recheck measurements.

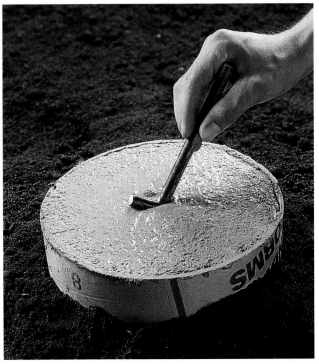

11 Insert a J-bolt at an angle into the wet concrete at center of the footing.

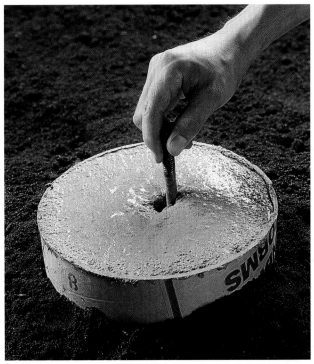

12 Lower the J-bolt slowly into the concrete, wiggling it slightly to eliminate any air gaps.

13 Set the J-bolt so ¾" to 1" is exposed above concrete. Brush away any wet concrete on bolt threads with an old toothbrush.

14 Use a plumb bob to make sure the J-bolt is positioned exactly at center of post location.

15 Use a torpedo level to make sure the J-bolt is plumb. If necessary, adjust the bolt and re-pack concrete. Let concrete cure, then cut away exposed portion of tube with a utility knife.

Setting Posts

Posts support the deck beams and transfer the weight of the deck to the concrete footings. For maximum strength, the posts must be plumb.

To prevent rot or insect damage, use pressure-treated lumber for posts, and make sure the factory-treated end faces down.

Use metal post anchors to attach the posts to the concrete footings. Post anchors have drainage holes and pedestals that raise the ends of the wood posts above the concrete footings.

Everything You Need:

Tools (page 30): pencil, framing square, ratchet wrench, tape measure, power miter box or circular saw, hammer, screwgun, level, combination square.

Materials: metal post anchors, nuts for J-bolts, lumber for posts, 6d galvanized common nails, 2" wallboard screws.

Supplies: long, straight 2 × 4; 1 × 4s; pointed 2 × 2 stakes.

How to Attach Post Anchors

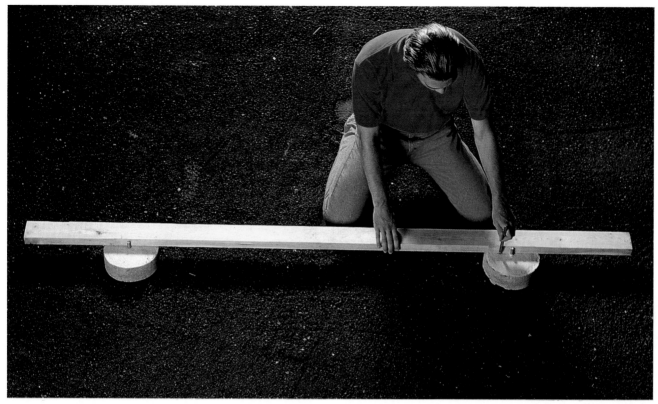

1 Mark the top of each footing as a reference line for installing post anchors. Lay a long, straight 2 × 4 flat across two or three concrete footings, parallel to the ledger, with one edge tight against the J-bolts.

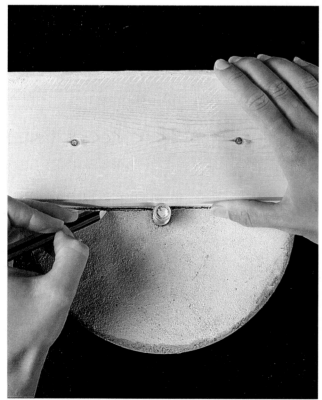

2 Draw a reference line across each concrete footing, using the edge of the 2 × 4 as a guide. Remove the 2 × 4.

3 Place a metal post anchor on each concrete footing, and center it over the J-bolt.

(continued next page)

How to Attach Post Anchors (continued)

4 Use a framing square to make sure the post anchor is positioned square to the reference line drawn on the footing.

5 Thread a nut over each J-bolt, and tighten it securely with a ratchet wrench.

How to Set Posts

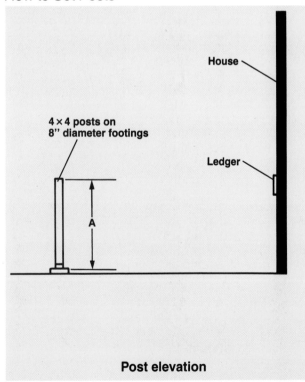

4 × 4 posts on 8" diameter footings

House

Ledger

A

Post elevation

1 Use the elevation drawing from the design plan (page 39) to find the length of each post (A). Add 6" for a cutting margin.

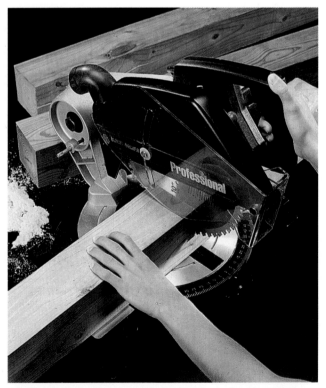

2 Cut posts with power miter box or circular saw. Make sure factory-treated ends of posts are square. If necessary, square them by trimming with a power miter box or circular saw.

3 Place post in anchor, and tack into place with a single 6d galvanized common nail.

4 Brace post with a 1 × 4. Place the 1 × 4 flat across post, so that it crosses the post at a 45° angle about halfway up.

5 Attach the brace to the post temporarily with a single 2'' wallboard screw.

6 Drive a pointed 2 × 2 stake into the ground next to the end of the brace.

(continued next page)

7 Use a level to make sure the post is plumb. Adjust the post, if necessary.

8 Attach the brace to the stake with two 2" wallboard screws.

9 Plumb and brace the post on the side perpendicular to the first brace.

10 Attach the post to the post anchor with 6d galvanized common nails.

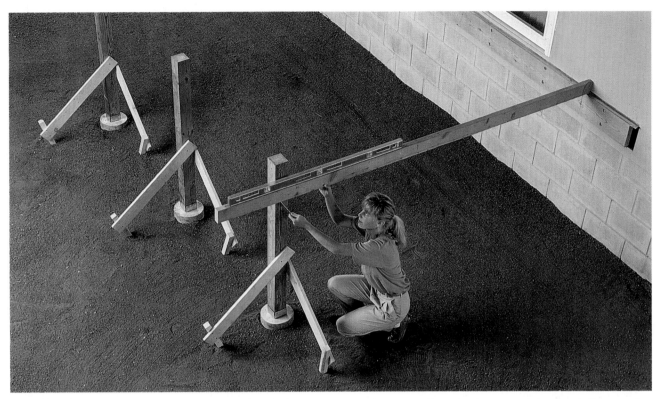

11 Position a straight 2 × 4 with one end on ledger and other end across face of post. Level the 2 × 4, then lower its post end ¼" for every 3 ft. between ledger and post (for water runoff) Draw a line on the post along the bottom of the 2 × 4. For cantilevered construction (pages 68 to 70), this line indicates the top of the joists. For corner-post construction (page 71), this line indicates the top of the beam.

12 For cantilevered construction, draw a line as shown in step 11. Then measure down a distance equal to width of joists, and mark the post.

13 Use a square to draw a line completely around the post. This line indicates the top of the canti-lever beam.

Installing a Beam

A deck beam is attached to the posts, and helps support the weight of the joists and decking. The method for installing the beam depends on whether the deck is a cantilevered or corner-post design.

A **cantilevered deck** has posts and one or more beams that are set back from the edge of the deck. The advantage is a neater and more attractive appearance. In cantilevered construction, the joists run across and extend past the beam. The general rule is the overhanging, or cantilevered, portion of the deck may be one-third the total length of the joists.

A **corner-post deck** has posts that are set at the edge of the deck. Because joists butt into the beam, rather than run across the top, corner-post construction is ideal for low decks.

Everything You Need:

Tools (page 30): tape measure, pencil, circular saw, paint brush, combination square, screwgun, drill, twist bits (⅛", ¼"), 1" spade bit, ratchet wrench, caulk gun, reciprocating saw or handsaw.

Materials: pressure-treated lumber, clear sealer-preservative, 2½" corrosion-resistant deck screws, ⅜" × 4" lag screws and 1" washers, ⅜" × 5" lag screws (for corner-post deck), silicone caulk.

How to Install a Beam for a Cantilevered Deck

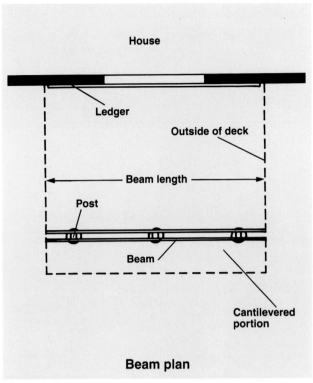

Beam plan

1 Use the deck design plan (page 38) to find the beam length. In plan shown above, the cantilever beam is cut to match overall width of deck.

2 Measure and mark two straight pressure-treated boards to length. Cut boards with a circular saw. Seal cut ends with clear sealer-preservative.

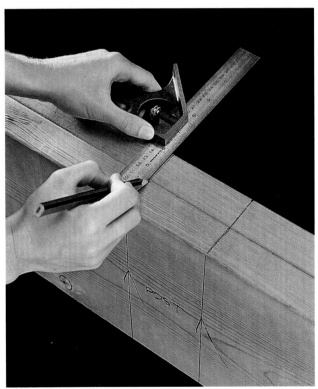

3 Hold beam boards together. Measure and mark the post locations on the tops and sides of boards, using a combination square as a guide.

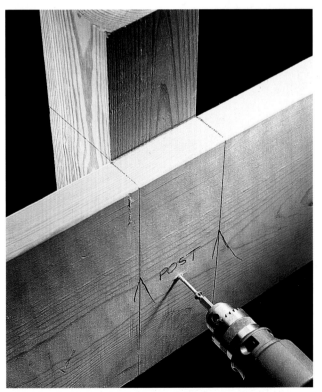

4 Position one beam board against the sides of the posts with crown side up. Marks on the board should be aligned with beam height marks on posts. Hold board in position with 2½" deck screws.

(continued next page)

5 Drill two ¼" pilot holes through the beam board and into each of the posts.

6 Counterbore each pilot hole to ½" depth, using 1" spade bit.

7 Attach board to posts with ⅜" × 4" lag screws and washers, using a ratchet wrench.

8 Attach the remaining beam board to the opposite sides of the posts, repeating steps 4 to 7. Seal screw heads with silicone caulk.

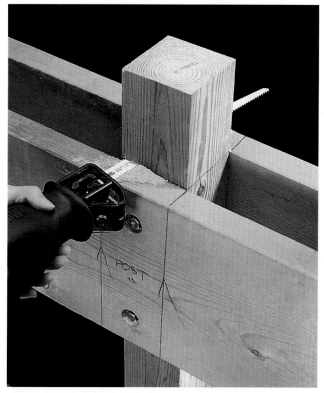

9 Cut tops of posts flush with top edge of beam, using a reciprocating saw or handsaw. Seal cut ends of posts with clear sealer-preservative.

How to Install a Beam for a Corner-post Deck

Beam plan

Labels: House, Ledger, Beam, Post, A, B

1 Use deck design plan (page 38) to find length of beam. Measure distance (A) between outside edges of corner posts. Mark pressure-treated board to length and cut with circular saw. Cut a second beam board (B), 3" longer than first board. Seal cut ends with clear sealer-preservative.

2 Position shorter beam board against outside of posts so that ends are flush with post edges. Top edge of board should be flush with beam height marks on posts. Drill ⅛" pilot holes, and hold beam board in position with 2½" deck screws.

3 Position the longer beam board against outside of the first board, so that ends overhang by 1½" to allow for outside joists. Fasten boards together with a pair of 2½" deck screws driven every 2 feet.

4 Drill two ¼" pilot holes through both beam boards and into each post. Counterbore each pilot hole to ½" depth, using a 1" spade bit. Secure boards to posts with ⅜" × 5" lag screws and washers, using a ratchet wrench. Seal screw heads and crack between boards with silicone caulk.

Hanging Joists

Joists provide support for the decking boards. In cantilever construction, joists are attached to the ledger and header joist with galvanized metal joist hangers, and are nailed to the top of the beam. In corner-post construction, joists are attached to the ledger and inside of the beam with galvanized joist hangers.

For strength and durability, use pressure-treated lumber for all joists. The exposed outside joists and header joist can be faced with redwood or cedar boards for a more attractive appearance (page 81).

Everything You Need:

Tools (page 30): tape measure, pencil, hammer, combination square, circular saw, paint brush, drill, twist bits (1⁄16", 1⁄4"), 1" spade bit.

Materials: pressure-treated lumber, clear sealer-preservative, 10d galvanized common nails, 1¼" joist nails, joist angle brackets, galvanized metal joist hangers, 3⁄8" × 4" lag screws and 1" washers.

How to Hang Joists

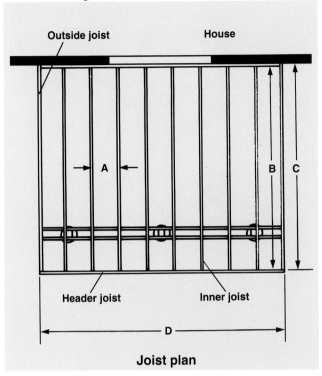

Joist plan

1 Use the design plan (page 38) to find the spacing (A) between joists, and the length of inner joists (B), outside joists (C), and header joist (D). Measure and mark lumber for outside joists, using a combination square as a guide. Cut joists with a circular saw. Seal cut ends with clear sealer-preservative.

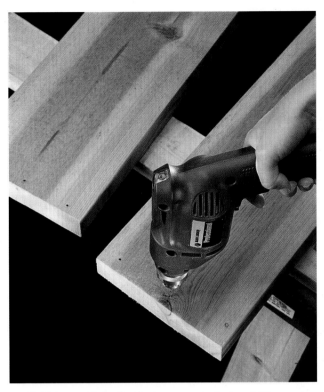

2 Drill three 1/16" pilot holes, spaced about 3" apart, through one end of each outside joist.

3 Hold the outside joists in position at ends of ledger with 10d nails driven into the ledger.

4 Attach the outside joists to the top of the beam by toenailing them with 10d nails.

(continued next page)

5 Measure and cut header joist. Seal cut ends with clear sealer-preservative. Drill 1/16'' pilot holes at each end of header joist. Attach header to ends of outside joists with 10d galvanized nails.

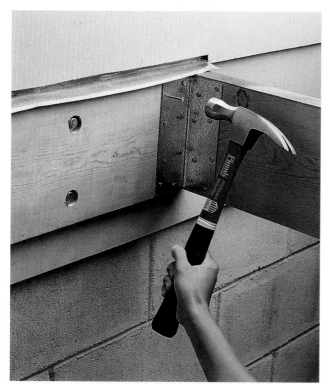

6 Strengthen each inside corner of the deck frame with an angle bracket. Attach the brackets with 1¼'' joist nails.

Alternate for corner-post deck: Position outside joist against post, flush with end of beam. Drill ¼'' pilot holes through end of joist, into post. Counterbore pilot holes to depth of ½''; using 1'' spade bit. Attach with ⅜'' × 4'' lag screws and washers. Cut off posts flush with top of beam, using a reciprocating saw or handsaw.

7 Measure along ledger from edge of outside joist, and mark where joists will be attached to ledger.

8 Draw the outline of each joist on the ledger, using a combination square as a guide.

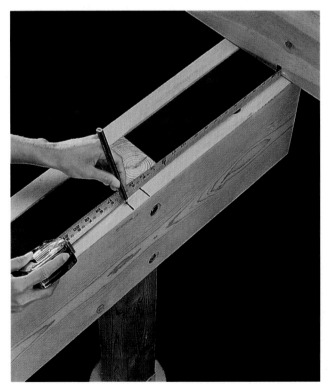

9 Measure along the beam from outside joist, and mark where joists will cross beam. Draw the outlines across top of both beam boards.

10 Measure along the header joist from the outside joist, and mark where joists will be attached to header joist. Draw the outlines on the inside of the header, using a combination square as a guide.

(continued next page)

11 Attach joist hangers to the ledger and to the header joist. Position each hanger so that one of the flanges is against the joist outline. Nail flange to framing member with 1¼" joist nails.

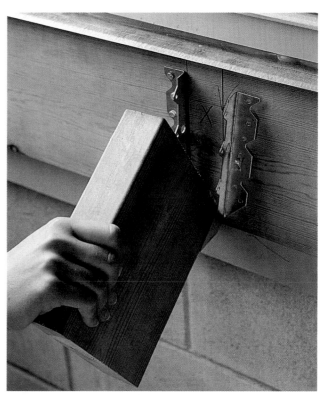

12 Cut a scrap board to use as a spacer. Hold spacer inside each joist hanger, then close the hanger around the spacer.

13 Nail the remaining side flange to the framing member with 1¼" joist nails. Remove spacer.

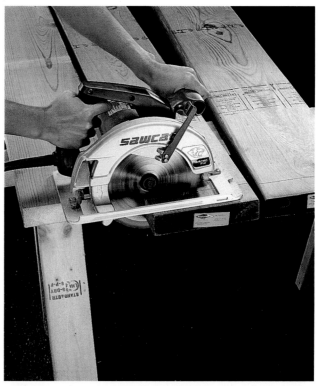

14 Measure and mark lumber for joists, using a combination square as a guide. Cut joists with a circular saw.

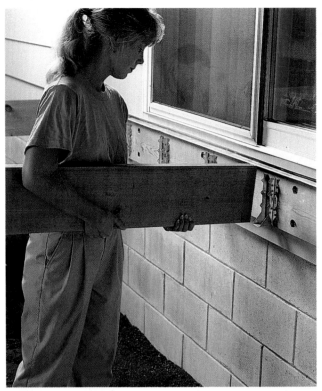

15 Seal cut ends with clear sealer-preservative. Place joists in hangers with crowned side up.

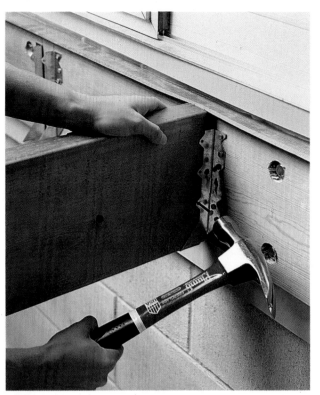

16 Attach the ledger joist hangers to the joists with 1¼" joist nails. Drive nails into both sides of each joist.

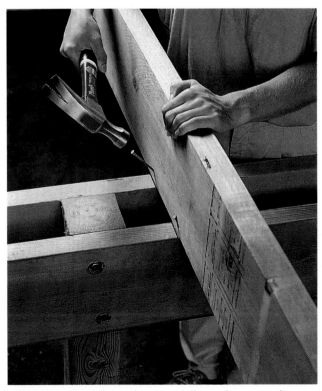

17 Align the joists with the outlines drawn on the top of the beam. Anchor the joists to the beam by toe-nailing from both sides with 10d galvanized nails.

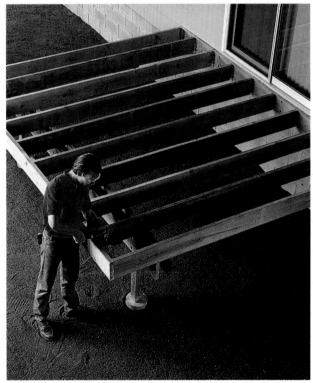

18 Attach the joists to the header joist hangers with 1¼" joist nails. Drive nails into both sides of each joist.

Laying Decking

Buy decking boards that are long enough to span the width of the deck, if possible. If boards must be butted end-to-end, make sure to stagger the joints so they do not overlap from row to row. Predrill the ends of boards to prevent screws or nails from splitting the wood.

Install decking so that there is a ⅛" gap between boards to provide drainage. Boards naturally "cup" as they age (page 21). Lay boards with the bark side facing down, so that the cupped surface cannot hold standing water.

Everything You Need:

Tools (page 30): tape measure, circular saw, screwgun, hammer, drill, ⅛" twist bit, pry bar, chalk line, jig saw or handsaw

Materials: decking boards, 2½" corrosion-resistant deck screws, galvanized common nails (8d, 10d), redwood or cedar facing boards.

1 Position the first row of decking flush against the house. First decking board should be perfectly straight, and should be precut to proper length. Attach the first decking board by driving a pair of 2½" corrosion-resistant deck screws into each joist.

2 Position remaining decking boards so that ends overhang outside joists. Space boards about ⅛" apart. Attach boards to each joist with a pair of 2½' deck screws driven into each joist.

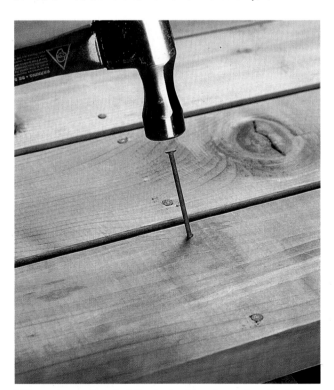

Alternate method: Attach decking boards with 10d galvanized common nails. Angle the nails toward each other to improve holding power.

(continued next page)

3 If boards are bowed, use a pry bar to lever them into position while fastening.

4 Drill ⅛" pilot holes in ends of boards before attaching them to outside joists. Pilot holes prevent screws from splitting decking boards at ends.

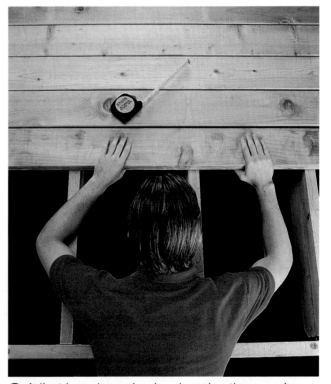

5 After every few rows of decking are installed, measure from edge of the decking board to edge of header joist. If measurements show that the last board will not fit flush against the edge of the deck, adjust board spacing.

6 Adjust board spacing by changing the gaps between boards by a small amount over three or four rows of boards. Very small spacing changes will not be obvious to the eye.

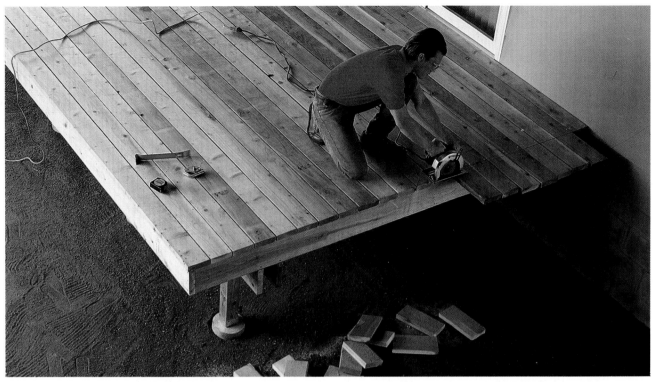

7 Use a chalk line to mark the edge of decking flush with the outside edge of deck. Cut off decking with a circular saw. Set saw blade ⅛" deeper than thickness of decking so that saw will not cut side of deck. At areas where circular saw cannot reach, finish cutoff with a jig saw or handsaw.

8 For a more attractive appearance, face the deck with redwood or cedar facing boards. Miter-cut corners, and attach boards with deck screws or 8d galvanized nails.

Alternate facing technique: Attach facing boards so that edges of decking overhang facing.

Building Stairs

Building deck stairs requires four calculations.

Number of steps depends on the vertical drop of the deck. The vertical drop is the distance from the surface of the deck to the ground.

Rise is the vertical space between treads. Building codes require that the rise measurement be about 7".

Run is the depth of the treads. A convenient way to build deck stairs is to use a pair of 2 × 6s for each tread.

Span is figured by multiplying the run by the number of treads. The span lets you locate the end of the stairway, and position support posts.

Everything You Need:

Tools (page 30): tape measure, pencil, framing square, level, plumb bob, posthole digger, wheelbarrow, hoe, circular saw, hammer, drill, ⅛" twist bit, 1" spade bit, ratchet wrench, caulk gun.

Materials: sand, portland cement, gravel, J-bolts, metal post anchors, 2 × 12 lumber, metal cleats, ¼" × 1¼" lag screws, joist angle brackets, 1¼" galvanized joist nails, ⅜" × 4" lag screws and 1" washers, 2 × 6 lumber, 16d nails, silicone caulk.

Supplies: long, straight 2 × 4; pointed stakes; masking tape.

Side stair elevation

Post
Railing
Post
Run (tread depth)
Stringer
2 × 6 treads
Vertical rise
18"
Span

Front stair elevation

Railing cap
Surface of deck
Stringer
Vertical rise
Post
2 × 6 treads
Metal cleats
Vertical drop

A deck stairway is made from two 2 × 12 stringers, and a series of treads attached with metal cleats. Posts set 18" back from the end of the stairway help to anchor the stringers and the railings. Calculations needed to build stairs include the **number of steps**, the **rise** of each step, the **run** of each step, and the stairway **span**.

How to Find Measurements for Stairway Layout

Sample Measurements
(39" High Deck)

1. Find the number of steps: Measure vertical drop from deck surface to ground. Divide by 7. Round off to nearest whole number.	Vertical drop:			39"
	÷ 7 =			5.57"
	Number of steps:	=	=	6
2. Find step rise: Divide the vertical drop by the number of steps.	Vertical drop:			39"
	Number of steps:	÷	÷	6
	Rise:	=	=	6.5"
3. Find step run: Typical treads made from two 2 × 6s have a run of 11¼". If your design is different, find run by measuring depth of tread, including any space between boards.	Run:			11¼"
4. Find stairway span: Multiply the run by the number of treads. (Number of treads is always one less than number of steps.)	Run:			11¼"
	Number of treads:	×	×	5
	Span:	=	=	56¼"

How to Build Deck Stairs

1 Use the stairway elevation drawings (page 83) to find measurements for stair stringers and posts. Use a pencil and framing square to outline where stair stringers will be attached to the side of the deck.

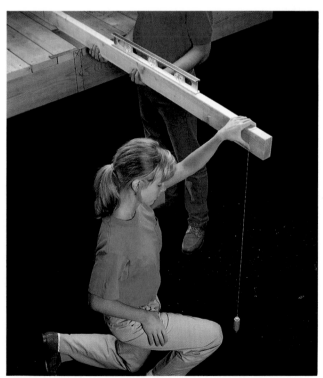

2 Locate the post footings so they are 18" back from the end of stairway span. Lay a straight 2 × 4 on the deck so that it is level and square to side of deck. Use a plumb bob to mark the ground at centerpoints of footings.

3 Dig holes and pour footings for posts (pages 58 to 61). Attach metal post anchors to footings and install 4 × 4 posts (pages 62 to 67).

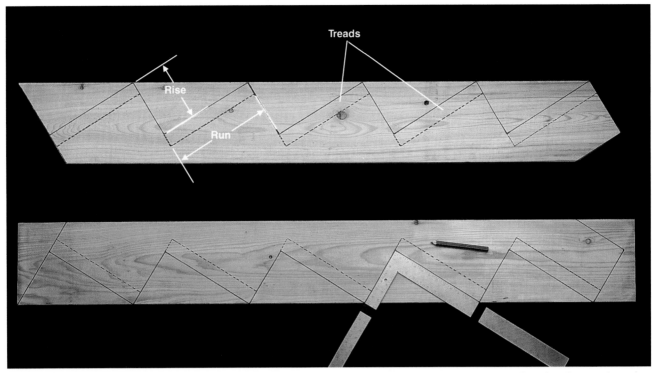

Treads

Rise

Run

4 Lay out stair stringers. Use tape to mark the rise measurement on one leg of a framing square, and the run measurement on the other leg. Beginning at one end of stringer, position the square with tape marks flush to edge of board, and outline the rise and run for each step. Then draw in the tread outline against the bottom of each run line. Use a circular saw to trim ends of stringers as shown.

5 Attach metal tread cleats flush with bottom of each tread outline, using ¼" × 1¼" lag screws. Drill ⅛" pilot holes to prevent the screws from splitting the wood.

6 Attach angle brackets to upper ends of stringers, using 1¼" joist nails. Brackets should be flush with cut ends of stringers.

(continued next page)

7 Position the stair stringers against side of deck, over the stringer outlines. Align top point of stringer flush with the surface of the deck. Attach stringers by nailing the angle brackets to the deck with 1¼" joist nails.

8 Drill two ¼" pilot holes through each stringer and into each adjacent post. Counterbore each hole to depth of ½", using a 1" spade bit. Attach stringers to posts with ⅜" × 4" lag screws and washers, using a ratchet wrench. Seal screw heads with silicone caulk.

9 Measure width of stair treads. Cut two 2 × 6s for each tread, using a circular saw.

10 For each step, position the front 2 × 6 on the tread cleat, so that the front edge is flush with the tread outline on the stringers.

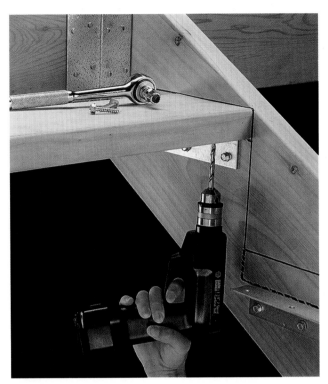

11 Drill ⅛" pilot holes, then attach the front 2 × 6s to the cleats with ¼" × 1¼" lag screws.

12 Position the rear 2 × 6s on the cleats, allowing a small space between boards. Use a 16d nail as a spacing guide. Drill ⅛" pilot holes, and attach 2 × 6s to cleats with ¼" × 1¼" lag screws.

Stair Variations

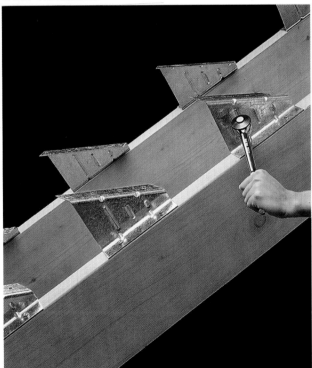

Hardware option: Metal step brackets can be attached to tops of stringers. This method allows the treads to overhang at the sides.

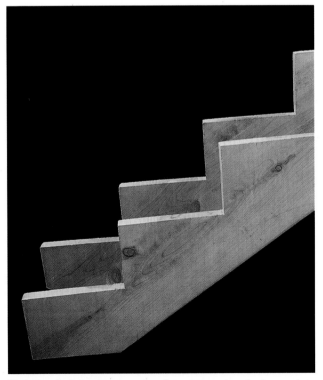

Notched stringers made of pressure-treated wood are available precut at building centers. Edges of cut-out areas should be coated with sealer-preservative to prevent rot.

Installing a Deck Railing

Railings must be sturdy, and should be firmly attached to the framing members of the deck. Never attach railing posts to the surface decking. Check local building codes for guidelines regarding railing construction. Most codes require that railings be at least 34" above decking. Vertical balusters should be spaced less than 6" apart.

Everything You Need:

Tools (page 30): tape measure, pencil, power miter box, drill, ¼" twist bits (⅛", ¼"), 1" spade bit, combination square, awl, ratchet wrench, caulk gun, level, reciprocating saw or circular saw, jig saw with wood-cutting blade.

Materials: railing lumber (4 × 4s, 2 × 6s, 2 × 4s, 2 × 2s), clear sealer-preservative, ⅜" × 4" lag screws and 1" washers, silicone caulk, 2½" corrosion-resistant deck screws, 10d galvanized common nails.

How to Install a Deck Railing

Railing detail

1 Refer to the deck design plan (pages 38 to 39) for spacing (A) and length of railing posts and balusters. Posts should be spaced no more than 6 feet apart.

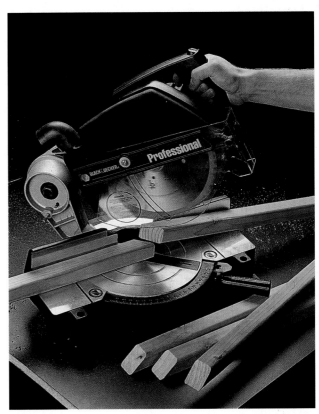

2 Measure and cut 4 × 4 posts, using a power miter box or circular saw. Cut off tops of the posts square, and cut the bottoms at 45° angle. Seal cut ends of lumber with clear sealer-preservative.

3 Measure and cut balusters for main deck, using a power miter box or circular saw. Cut off tops of the balusters square, and cut bottoms at 45° angle. Seal cut ends of lumber with clear sealer-preservative.

4 Drill two ¼" pilot holes through bottom end of each post, spaced 4" apart. Counterbore each pilot hole to ½" depth, using a 1" spade bit.

5 Drill two ⅛" pilot holes near bottom end of each baluster, spaced 4" apart. Drill two ⅛" pilot holes at top of each baluster, spaced 1½" apart.

(continued next page)

6 Measure and mark position of posts around the outside of the deck, using a combination square as a guide. Plan to install a post on outside edge of each stair stringer.

7 Position each post with beveled end flush with bottom of deck. Plumb post with a level. Insert a screwdriver or nail into pilot holes and mark side of deck.

8 Remove post and drill ¼" pilot holes into side of deck.

9 Attach railing posts to side of deck with ⅜" × 4" lag screws and washers, using a ratchet wrench. Seal screw heads with silicone caulk.

10 Measure and cut 2 × 4 side rails. Position rails with edges flush to tops of posts, and attach to posts with 2½" corrosion-resistant deck screws.

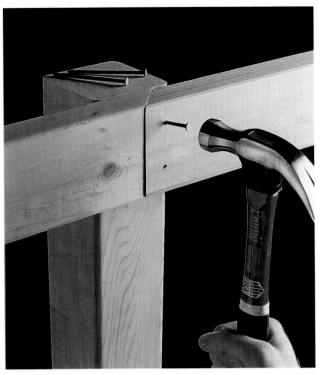

11 Join 2 × 4s for long rails by cutting ends at 45° angle. Drill 1/16'' pilot holes to prevent nails from splitting end grain, and attach rails with 10d galvanized nails. (Screws may split mitered ends.)

12 Attach ends of rails to stairway posts, flush with edges of posts, as shown. Drill 1/8'' pilot holes, and attach rails with 2½'' deck screws.

13 At stairway, measure from surface of decking to the top of the upper stairway post (A).

14 Transfer measurement A to lower stairway post, measuring from the edge of the stair stringer.

(continued next page)

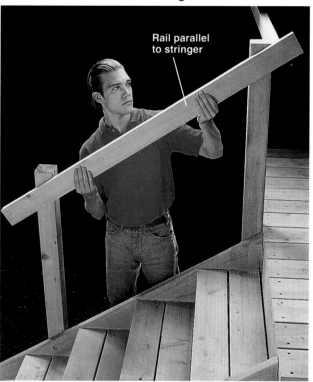

15 Position 2 × 4 rail against inside of stairway posts. Align rail with top rear corner of top post, and with the pencil mark on the lower post. Have a helper attach rail temporarily with 2½" deck screws.

16 Mark the outline of the post and the deck rail on the back side of the stairway rail.

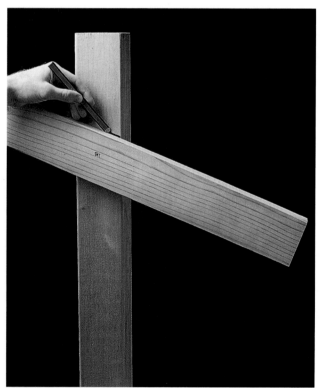

17 Mark the outline of the stairway rail on the lower stairway post.

18 Use a level to mark a plumb cutoff line at the bottom end of the stairway rail. Remove the rail.

19 Extend the pencil lines across both sides of the stairway post, using a combination square as a guide.

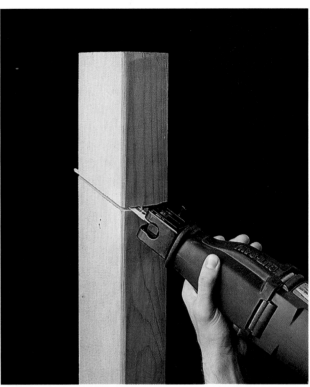

20 Cut off lower stairway post along diagonal cutoff line, using a reciprocating saw or circular saw.

21 Use a jig saw to cut the stairway rail along the marked outlines.

22 Position the stairway rail flush against top edge of posts. Drill 1/8" pilot holes, then attach rail to posts with 2½" deck screws.

(continued next page)

23 Use a spacer block to ensure equal spacing between balusters. Beginning next to a plumb railing post, position each baluster tight against spacer block, with top of baluster flush to top of rail. Attach each baluster with 2½" deck screws.

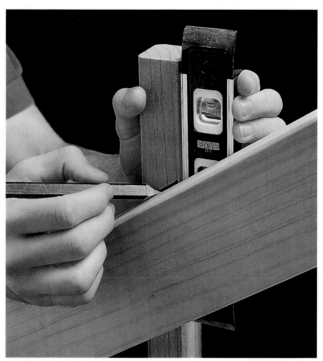

24 For stairway, position baluster against stringer and rail, and adjust for plumb. Draw diagonal cutoff line on top of baluster, using top of stair rail as a guide. Cut baluster on marked line, using power miter box. Seal ends with clear sealer-preservative.

25 Beginning next to upper stairway post, position each baluster tight against spacer block, with top flush to top of stair rail. Attach baluster with 2½" deck screws.

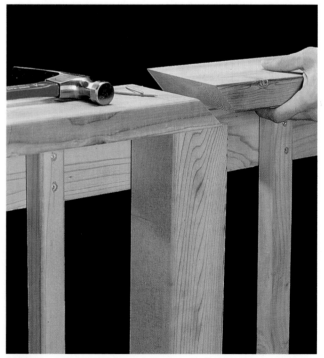

26 Position 2 × 6 cap so edge is flush with inside edge of rail. Drill ⅛" pilot holes, and attach cap to rail with 2½" deck screws driven every 12". Also drive screws into each post and into every third baluster. For long caps, bevel ends at 45°. Drill ¹⁄₁₆" pilot holes, and attach at post using 10d nails.

27 At corners, miter ends of railing cap at 45°. Drill ⅛" pilot holes, and attach cap to post with 2½" deck screws.

28 At top of stairs, cut cap so that it is flush with stairway rail. Drill ⅛" pilot holes and attach cap with 2½" deck screws.

29 Measure and cut cap for stairway rail. Mark outline of post on side of cap, and bevel-cut the ends of the cap.

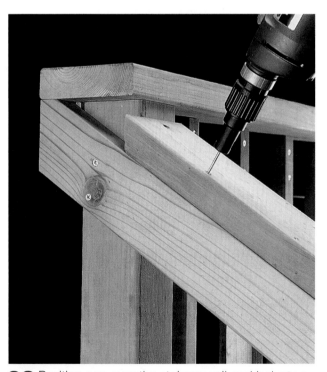

30 Position cap over the stairway rail and balusters so that edge of cap is flush with inside edge of rail. Drill ⅛" pilot holes, and attach cap to rail with 2½" deck screws driven every 12". Also drive screws through cap into stair post and into every third baluster.

Platform Deck

A platform deck is built low to the ground, so it is ideal for a flat, level yard, and when the height of the interior floor is close to the surface of the yard.

Because it is low to the ground, a platform deck does not require railings or stairs. It has an open, airy feeling that makes it an ideal place for sunning or entertaining.

The platform deck shown at left adds visual interest with a second level and redwood decking laid on the diagonal. The decking is a mix of cream-colored sapwood, and reddish heartwood that is rot-resistant. Always treat sapwood with a clear sealer-preservative.

A redwood facing board runs around the edges of this deck. Redwood that comes in contact with the ground or with grass should be treated with a clear sealer-preservative before installation.

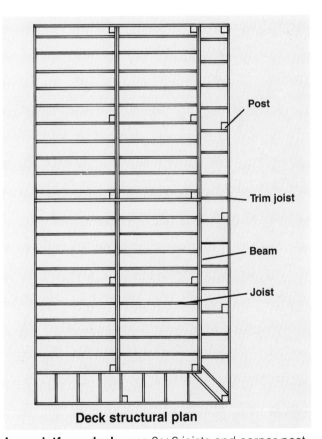

Deck structural plan

Low platform deck uses 2 × 6 joists and corner-post beams that require closely spaced posts for extra support. Joists for interior portion of deck are spaced 12" on-center to support longer spans of diagonal decking. Short joists (called trim joists) around the perimeter of the deck support the border decking boards.

Photo courtesy of the California Redwood Association

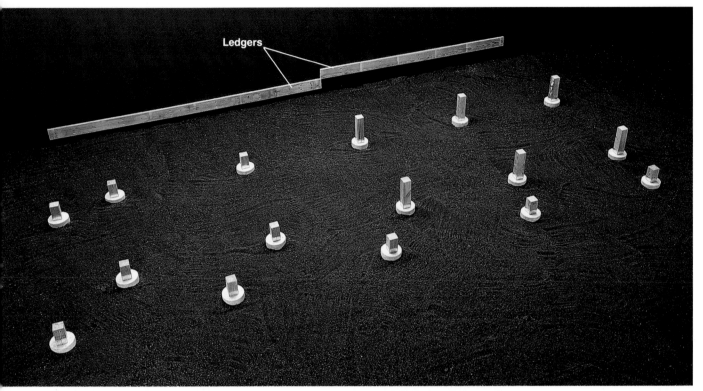

Ledgers

1 Attach 2 × 6 pressure-treated ledgers to house with ⅜" × 4" lag screws (pages 46 to 51). Pour footings and install 4 × 4 pressure-treated posts (pages 58 to 67). Mark posts to indicate tops of beams.

2 Build each beam from a pair of pressure-treated 2 × 6s (pages 68 to 71). Hold 2 × 6s together with 2½" corrosion-resistant deck screws driven every 18". Drill counterbored pilot holes and attach beams to posts with ⅜" × 5" lag screws. Cut all post tops flush with tops of beams.

3 Hang pressure-treated joists (pages 72 to 77). Lay out interior joists at 12" on-center. Install all joists with galvanized joist hangers and joist nails. Attach end joists to posts, not beams, with 2½" deck screws. End grain has little holding power.

4 Attach 2 × 6 pressure-treated outside joists and header joist to posts, using ⅜" × 3" lag screws (pages 73 to 74). Counterbore pilot holes so that facing boards can be installed. Reinforce inside corners of outside joists with angle brackets. Cut off all post tops flush with tops of header and outside joists.

(continued next page)

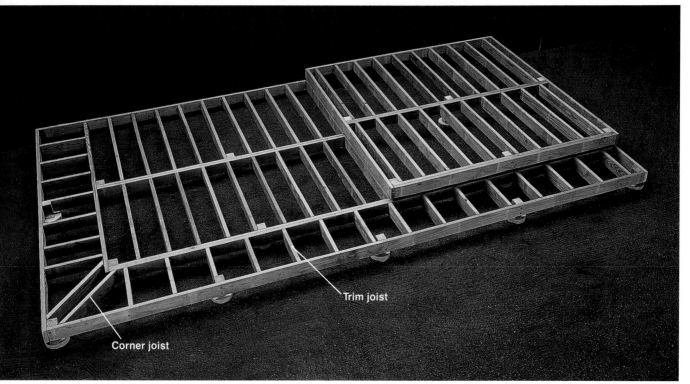

Trim joist

Corner joist

5 Lay out trim joists at 16" on-center. Attach the trim joists with galvanized joist hangers and joist nails. Cut the ends of the diagonal corner joists at a 45° angle, and install with angled joist hangers.

6 Install all diagonal decking (pages 78 to 81). Decking boards that will butt against the house should be pre-mitered at 45°. Use a chalk line to snap a cutoff line across the overhanging decking, flush with outside edges of beams and end joists. Cut off decking with circular saw with blade depth set to match thickness of decking.

Herringbone pattern

7 Install the decking border. Begin with board against diagonal pattern, and work toward outside edge of deck. Adjust spacing between decking so that the edge of the last board is exactly flush with edge of header or outside joist (page 80). Stagger the ends of the boards at corner to create a herringbone pattern, as shown.

Facing boards

8 Install facing boards (page 81). Top edge of facing should be flush with top of decking. For appearance, choose top-grade lumber for facing. Miter the corners at 45°, and fasten facing boards with 2½" corrosion-resistant deck screws driven every 18".

Photo courtesy of the California Redwood Association

Diamond-pattern Deck

Give your deck a distinct look with an unusual decking pattern. The visual appeal of a deck can be improved by using a diagonal or diamond-shaped decking pattern, like the one at left.

Install double joists or a row of double blocking for extra strength and stability wherever ends of decking boards butt together. Space the joists at 12" on-center to support the diagonal decking.

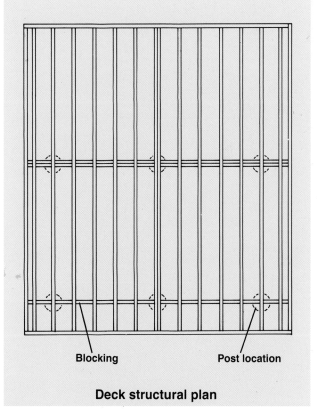

Blocking   **Post location**

Deck structural plan

Diamond-pattern deck has blocking added to provide surface for attaching ends of decking. Joist spacing on diagonal decking pattern is 12" on-center.

How to Build a Diamond-pattern Deck

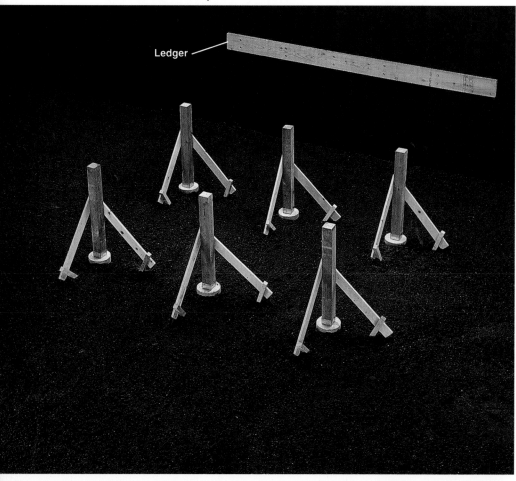

Ledger

1 Install pressure-treated ledger (pages 46 to 51).

Pour post footings and install 4 × 4 pressure-treated posts (pages 58 to 67). Seal all cut ends of lumber with sealer-preservative.

Brace all posts longer than 2 feet (pages 65 to 66).

Beam

2 Build each deck beam from pressure-treated lumber (pages 68 to 71). Position the boards against the row of posts, and drill a pair of ¼" pilot holes through boards and into each post. Attach the beam to the posts with ⅜" × 4" galvanized lag screws and washers.

Cut off all post tops flush with the top edges of the beams, using a reciprocating saw or handsaw.

3 Cut the header and outside joists from pressure-treated lumber.

Attach the outside joists to the ledger and to the tops of the beams, using 10d galvanized nails.

Attach the header joist to the ends of the outside joists, using 10d nails, then reinforce inside corners with angle brackets (page 74).

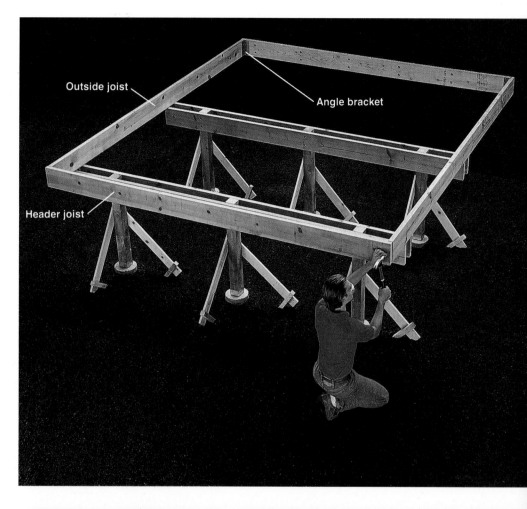

Outside joist

Angle bracket

Header joist

4 Hang the inside joists (pages 72 to 77).

Attach the joists to the ledger and header joist with galvanized metal joist hangers.

Install a double joist at the center of the framework to provide extra support where the ends of the decking boards will butt together.

Toenail all joists to the tops of the beams with 10d galvanized nails. Seal seam between double joists with silicone caulk.

Double joist

(continued next page)

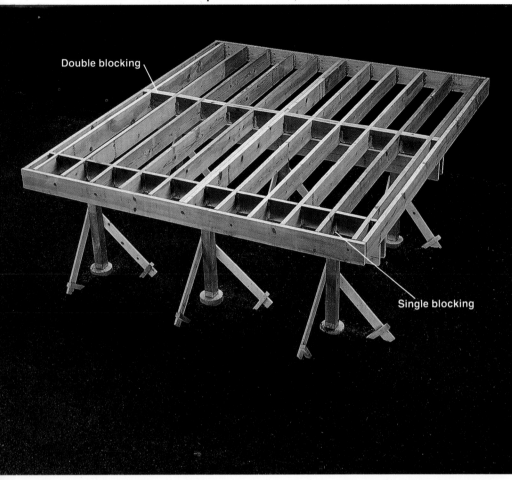

Double blocking

Single blocking

5 Install a row of double blocking between each pair of joists at the center of the diamond pattern, using galvanized joist hangers.

Install a row of single blocking at the end of the diamond pattern joist, using galvanized joist hangers. Blocking provides support where the ends of the diagonal decking boards form a continuous line.

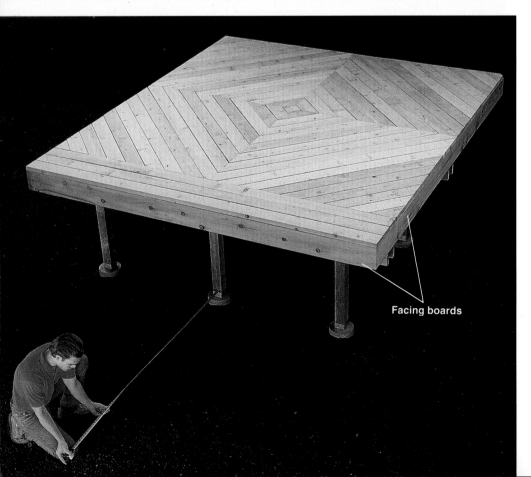

Facing boards

6 Face the header and outside joists with high-quality boards (page 81). Miter the corners of the boards at 45°, and attach with 8d galvanized nails.

Lay 2 × 6 redwood decking (pages 78 to 81). Use a combination square to mark the ends of angled boards at 45°, and cut with a circular saw or a power miter box.

Lay out the deck stairs (pages 82 to 83).

7 Pour stairway footings, and install post anchors and 4 × 4 posts.

Build the deck stairs (pages 82 to 87). The 2 × 10 stringers are attached to side of deck with ⅜" × 4" lag screws driven through back of header joist, and are anchored to the stairway posts with ⅜" × 4" lag screws.

Attach the stair treads to the stringers with metal cleats and lag screws.

8 Build post-and-baluster railing for the deck and stairway (pages 88 to 95).

Attach the 4 × 4 posts to the deck with ⅜" × 6" lag screws. Attach the 2 × 4 horizontal rails, the rail cap, and 2 × 2 balusters with 2½" corrosion-resistant deck screws. For a decorative detail, let posts and balusters extend below facing boards.

Island Deck

Build an island deck to create a sitting or dining area anywhere in your yard. Because an island deck is not attached to your house, it can be constructed to take advantage of afternoon shade patterns or scenic views.

Create visual interest with an octagonal deck. A short platform, or "gangway," gives access to the deck from three directions. An island deck may include pathways of brick or crushed rock that lead to the house.

Careful planning is usually required for decks with odd shapes, like an octagon. The eight-sided portion of the deck shown at right uses eight posts and four beams for complete stability.

Deck structural plan

Island deck has four beams and eight posts to create the support system for octagonal shape. Joists run at right angles to the decking. Outside joists are mitered at 22½° on an octagonal deck. Gangway platform is built using corner-post construction.

Photo by Lea Babcock

How to Build an Island Deck

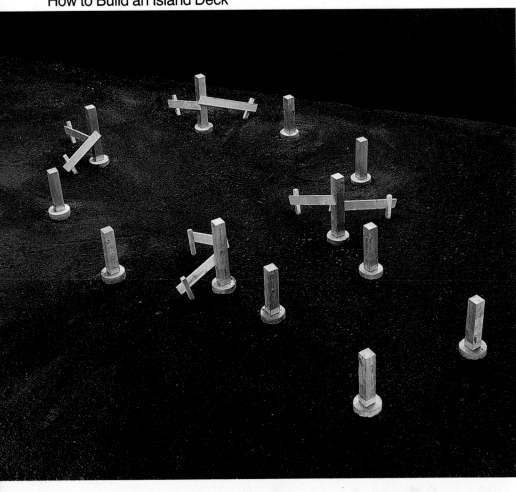

1 Pour post footings and install 4 × 4 pressure-treated posts (pages 58 to 67).

Plan deck layout so that there are eight posts for the main deck and four additional posts for the gangway.

The main portion of the deck uses cantilevered construction. Because the gangway is built low to the ground, use corner-post construction for this portion of the deck.

Posts longer than 2 feet should be braced plumb.

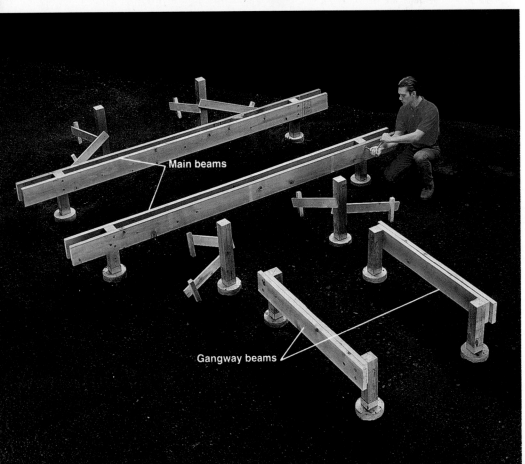

Main beams

Gangway beams

2 Build main beams from pressure-treated lumber (pages 68 to 71).

The two main beams for the octagonal deck run in the same direction as the decking boards. Build the beams for gangway using corner-post construction.

Attach the beams to the posts with ⅜" × 4" galvanized lag screws and washers.

Cut off the posts flush with the tops of the beams. Seal the cut ends with clear sealer-preservative.

3 Install two additional 2 × 8 beams across the main beams.

These beams are on the same level as the joists. Because they are attached directly to posts, these beams function as structural beams.

Cut off posts flush with the tops of the beams, and seal the ends with clear sealer-preservative.

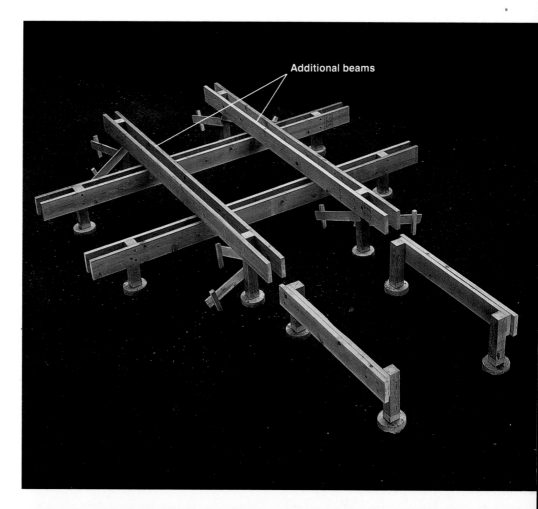

Additional beams

4 Attach all outside joists (page 74). The cutting angle for the ends of outside joists is 22½° on an octagonal deck.

Attach the outside joists to the additional beams with galvanized metal joist hangers.

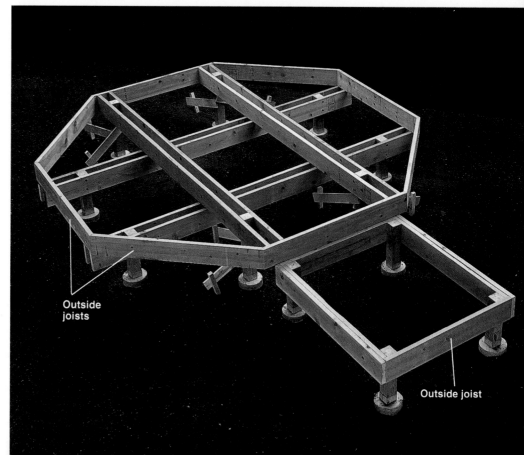

Outside joists

Outside joist

(continued next page)

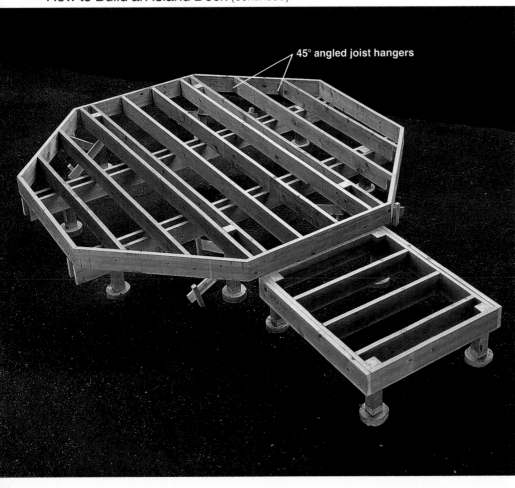

45° angled joist hangers

5 Hang pressure-treated inside joists (pages 75 to 77).

Install the joists parallel to the additional beams, using galvanized metal joist hangers.

Use 45° joist hangers for installing joists to angled outside joists.

Remove all post bracing.

6 Install all the decking using 2½'' corrosion-resistant deck screws (pages 78 to 81). Run the ends of the decking boards past all outside joists.

Use a chalk line to snap a cutting line on the decking, flush with the edges of the outside joists.

Cut decking using a circular saw with blade depth set to match thickness of the decking.

7 Face the outside edges of the deck with high-quality lumber for appearance.

Build deck stairs (pages 82 to 87). For stairways with three steps or less, railings may not be required. Consult local building codes.

The ends of stairway stringers may rest directly on a concrete sidewalk, patio paths, or the ground.

Seal all parts of the stairway with a clear sealer-preservative to prevent rot.

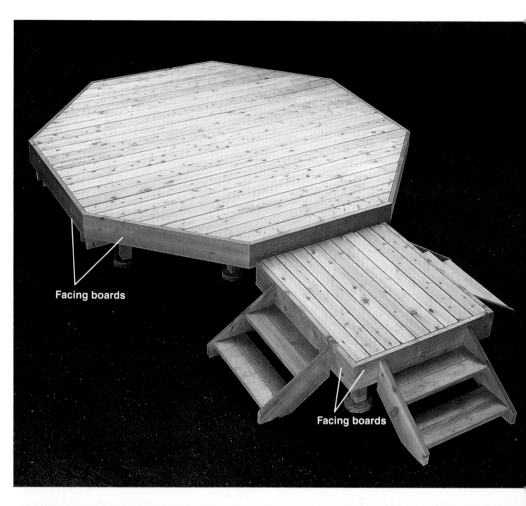

Facing boards

Facing boards

8 Install the post-and-baluster railings (pages 88 to 95). To support the handrail of an octagonal deck, use pairs of 2 × 4s at the corners instead of 4 × 4s. Use 2 × 2s for the balusters.

Install the 2 × 4s on edge, using ⅜" × 5" galvanized lag screws. The spacing between the 2 × 4s should be the same as that used between the 2 × 2 balusters.

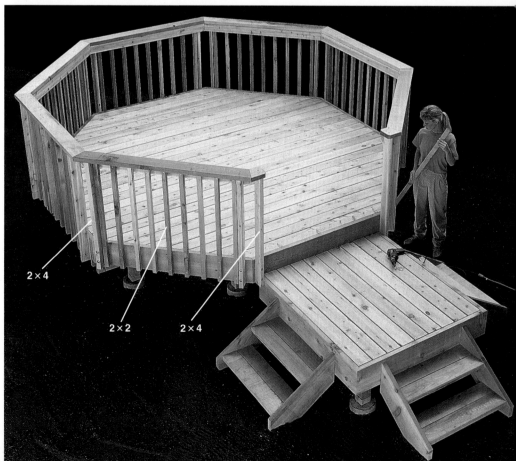

2 × 4

2 × 2   2 × 4

Deck Finishing & Repair

Finishing a New Deck

Finish a deck with clear sealer-preservative or staining sealer. Sealer-preservatives protect wood from water and rot, and are often used on cedar or redwood, because they preserve the original color of the wood. If you want the wood to look weathered, wait several months before applying sealer-preservative.

Staining sealers, sometimes called toners, are often applied to pressure-treated lumber to give it the look of redwood or cedar. Staining sealers are available in a variety of colors.

For best protection, use finishing products with an alkyd base. Apply fresh finish each year.

Everything You Need:

Tools: orbital sander, sandpaper, shop vacuum, pressure sprayer, eye protection, paint brush.

Materials: clear sealer-preservative or staining sealer.

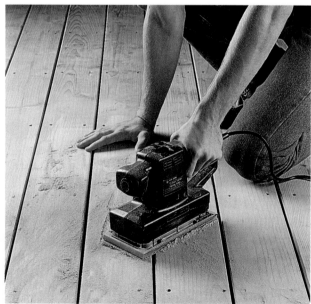

Use an orbital sander to smooth out any rough areas before applying finish to decking boards, railings, or stair treads.

How to Finish a Redwood or Cedar Deck

1 Test wood surface by sprinkling water on it. If wood absorbs water quickly, it is ready to be sealed. If wood does not absorb water, let it dry for several weeks before sealing.

2 Sand rough areas and vacuum deck. Apply clear sealer to all wood surfaces, using a pressure sprayer. If possible, apply sealer to underside of decking and to joists, beams, and posts.

3 Use a paint brush to work sealer into cracks and narrow areas that could trap water.

How to Finish a Pressure-treated Deck

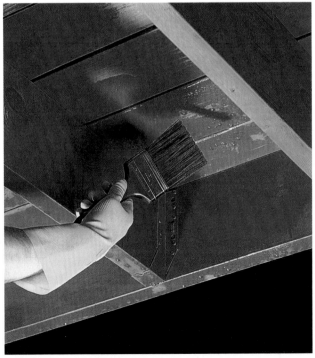

1 Sand rough areas and vacuum the deck. Apply a staining sealer (toner) to all deck wood, using a pressure sprayer.

2 Use a paint brush to smooth out drips and runs. Porous wood may require a second coat of staining sealer for even coverage.

Tips for Maintaining an Older Deck

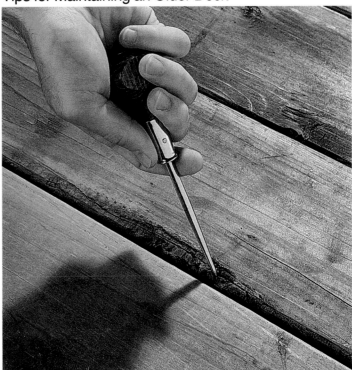

Use an awl or screwdriver to check deck for soft, rotted wood. Replace or reinforce damaged wood (pages 122 to 125).

How to Renew a Deck

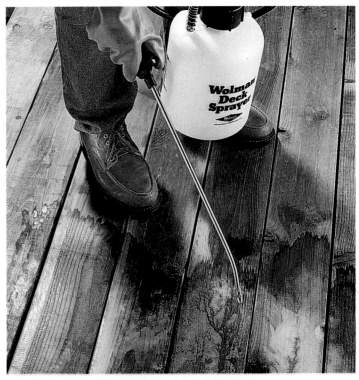

1 Mix deck-brightening solution as directed by manufacturer. Apply solution with pressure sprayer. Let solution set for 10 minutes.

Inspect hidden areas regularly for signs of rotted or damaged wood. Apply a fresh coat of finish yearly.

Maintaining a Deck

Inspect your deck once each year. Replace loose or rusting hardware or fasteners, and apply fresh finish to prevent water damage.

Look carefully for areas that show signs of damage. Replace or reinforce damaged wood as soon as possible (pages 122 to 125).

Restore an older, weathered deck to the original wood color with a deck-brightening solution. Brighteners are available at any home improvement store.

Everything You Need:

Tools: flashlight, awl or screwdriver, screwgun, putty knife, scrub brush, rubber gloves, eye protection, pressure sprayer.

Materials: 2½" corrosion-resistant deck screws, deck brightener.

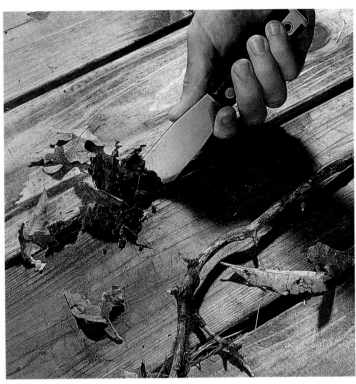

Clean debris from cracks between decking boards with a putty knife. Debris traps moisture, and can cause wood to rot.

Drive new fasteners to secure loose decking to joists. If using the old nail or screw holes, new fasteners should be slightly longer than the originals.

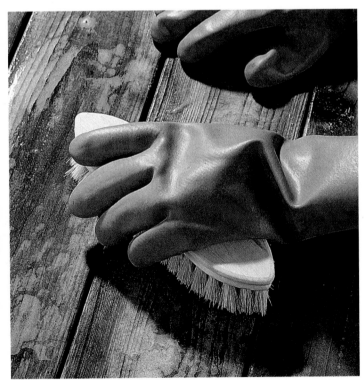

2 Scrub deck thoroughly with a stiff scrub brush. Wear rubber gloves and eye protection.

3 Rinse deck with clear water. If necessary, apply a second coat of brightener to extremely dirty or stained areas. Rinse and let dry. Apply a fresh coat of sealer or stain (page 118 to 119).

Repairing a Deck

Replace or reinforce damaged deck wood as soon as possible. Wood rot can spread and weaken solid wood.

After replacing or reinforcing the rotted wood, clean the entire deck and apply a fresh coat of clear sealer-preservative or staining sealer. Apply a fresh coat of finish each year to prevent future water damage.

Everything You Need:

Tools: cat's paw or flat pry bar, screwgun, awl or screwdriver, hammer, chisel, eye protection, pressure-sprayer, circular saw, scrub brush, paint brush, hydraulic jack, drill or hammer drill, ⅝" masonry bit, level, ratchet wrench.

Materials: sealer-preservative or staining sealer, galvanized nails (6d, 10d), deck lumber, baking soda, corrosion-resistant deck screws, ⅝" masonry anchor, ⅜" lag screw.

Supplies: rubber gloves, bucket, concrete block, scrap plywood.

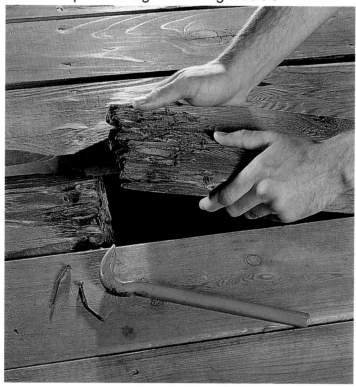

1 Remove nails or screws from the damaged decking board, using a cat's paw or screwgun. Remove the damaged board.

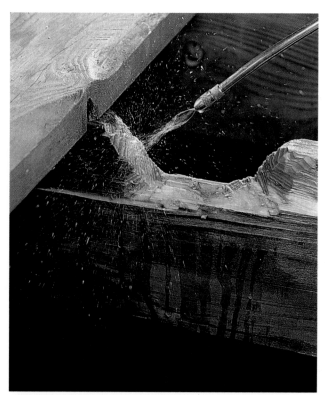

4 Apply a thick coat of sealer-preservative to damaged joist. Let dry, then apply a second coat of sealer. Cut a reinforcing joist (sister joist) from pressure-treated lumber.

5 Treat all sides of sister joist with clear sealer-preservative, and let dry. Position sister joist tightly against the damaged joist, and attach with 10d nails driven every 2 feet.

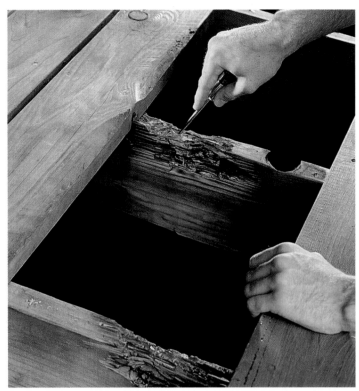

2 Inspect the underlying joists for signs of rotted wood. Joists with discolored, soft areas should be repaired and reinforced.

3 Use a hammer and chisel to remove any rotted portions of joist.

6 Attach sister joist to ledger and header joist by toenailing with 10d nails. Cut replacement decking boards from matching lumber, using a circular saw.

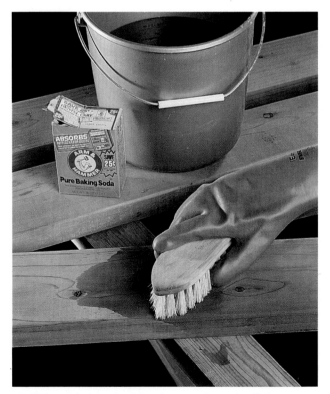

7 If the existing decking is gray, "weather" the new decking by scrubbing with a solution made from 1 cup baking soda and 1 gallon warm water. Rinse and let dry.

(continued next page)

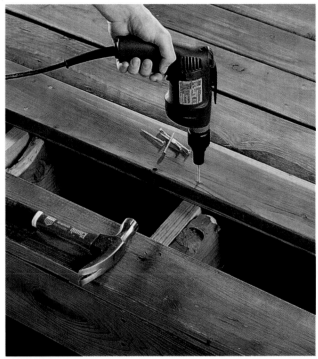

8 Apply a coat of sealer-preservative or staining sealer to all sides of the new decking board.

9 Position the new decking and attach to joists with galvanized deck screws or nails. Make sure space between boards matches that of existing decking.

How to Replace a Post on an Older Deck

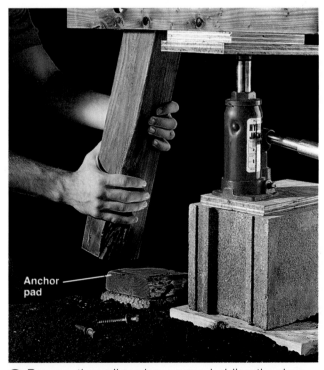

Anchor pad

1 Build a support, using plywood scraps, a concrete block, and a hydraulic jack. Place 1½" layer of plywood between head of jack and beam. Apply just enough pressure to lift the beam slightly.

2 Remove the nails or lag screws holding the damaged post to the anchor pad and to the beam. Remove the damaged post and the wood anchor pad on the concrete pier.

3 Drill a hole in the middle of the concrete pier, using a hammer drill and a ⅝" masonry bit. Insert ⅝" masonry anchor into hole.

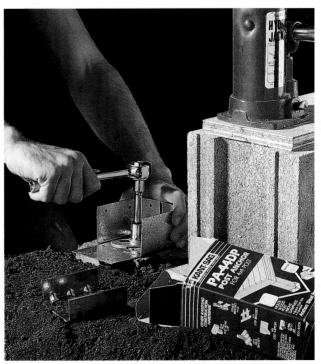

4 Position galvanized post anchor on pier block, and thread a ⅜" lag screw with washer through the hole in the anchor and into the masonry anchor. Tighten the screw with a ratchet wrench.

5 Cut new post from pressure-treated lumber, and treat cut ends with sealer-preservative. Position post and make sure it is plumb.

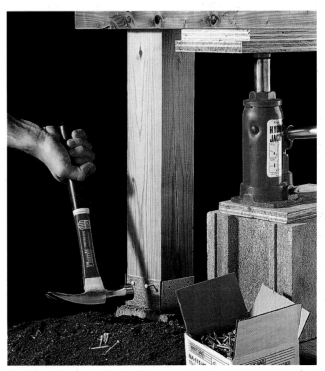

6 Attach the bottom of the post to the post anchor, using 6d galvanized nails. Attach the post to the beam by redriving the lag screws, using a ratchet wrench. Release the pressure on the jack and remove the support.

Index

A

Anchors,
  masonry, 27
  post, 27
Angle brackets, 27
  building stairs, 82, 85, 86
  hanging joists, 72, 74, 101, 107
Angled joist hangers, 27
Awl, 30, 120

B

Balusters, 14, 15, 19, 88, 89
Batterboards, 44, 52-57
Beams, 14, 45
  gangway, 112
  installation, 68-71
  plan for cantilever construction, 69
  plan for corner-post construction, 71
  size, 25
  span, 25
Blocking, 16, 17
Border decking pattern, 17
Boxed steps, 18
Brackets, angle, 27
Brightener, deck maintenance,
  120, 121
Building codes, 14, 18, 19, 58, 88, 115
Building Decks, 43-95
Building permit, 44
Building supplies, 40-41

C

Cantilevered deck,
  beam installation, 68-70
  beam plan, 69
  hanging joists, 72-77
  setting posts, 62-67
Cap, railing, 14, 15, 19
  size, 25
Carpenter's triangle, 55
Cat's paw, 30, 122
Caulk gun, 30
Caulking,
  beam installation, 68, 70
  building stairs, 82, 86
  ledger installation, 46, 48-51
  railing installation, 90
CCA (chromated copper arsenate),
  20, 22
Cedar, 14, 20, 22, 23
  facing boards, 81
  joists, 72
Cedar deck, finishing, 118-119
Chalk line, 30, 79, 81
Chisel, 30
  decking repair, 122-123
  ledger installation, 46-47
Circular saw, 31
Clamshell posthole digger, 30
  building stairs, 82
  digging footings, 58, 59
Claw hammer, 30, 52, 54
Cleats, 14, 18, 27, 82-83, 85, 87, 109
Combination square, 30
  beam installation, 68-69
  hanging joists, 72-73, 75
  railing installation, 90, 93
  setting posts, 62, 67

Compass, 30
Concrete, 28-29
  footings, 14, 58, 60-61, 82, 84
  tube forms, 58-61
Corner-post deck,
  beam installation, 68, 71
  beam plan, 71
  hanging joists, 72-77
  setting posts, 64-67

D

Deck Basics, 13-31
Deck building, overview, 44-45
Deck design, 36-39
Deck fasteners, 26
Deck Finishing & Repair, 117-125
Deck maintenance, 120-121
Deck parts, 14-15
Deck planning, 24-25, 34-41
Deck, renewing, 120-121
Deck repair, 122-125
Deck styles, 6-11
Decking, 14-15, 44
  boards, 25, 79
  facing, 81
  laying, 79-81
  patterns, 16-17
  repair, 122-124
  span, 25
Design & Planning, 33-41
Design plan, 36-39
  approval, 44
  beam installation, 69, 71
  joists, 73
  railing installation, 88
Diagonal decking pattern, 16, 105-109
Diamond-pattern deck, 16, 105-109
Digging footings, 58-61
Double joists, 16-17, 105, 107
Drill, 31

E

Elevation drawings,
  design, 34, 36, 39, 64
  post, 64
  site, 34-35
  stairway, 83
End grain, decking boards, 21
Eye protection, 22, 31

F

Facing boards, 14-15, 79, 81, 103,
  108, 115
Fasteners, 26-27

Feature Decks, 97-115
Finishing a deck, 118-119
Flashing, 27, 46, 48
Flat pry bar, 30
  deck repair, 122
Footings, 14, 44-45
  attaching post anchors, 62-64
  buying and mixing concrete, 28-29
  digging and pouring, 58-61
  locating, 52-57, 84
Framed opening, decking, 17
Framing square, 30
Freestanding deck, 11

G

Galvanized hardware, 26-27, 40
Gangway platform, 110-115
Grade stamp, 22, 23

H

Hammers, 30
  masonry, 52, 54, 56
Handrails, 19
Hardware, 26-27
Header joists, 14
  for diamond-pattern deck, 107
  hanging, 73-74
  ledger installation, 46, 48, 51
Heartwood, 20, 23
Herringbone decking pattern, 103
Hoe, 30
Hydraulic jack, 31
  deck repair, 122, 124-125

I

Installing a beam, 68-71
Installing a deck railing, 88-95
Installing the ledger, 46-51
Island deck, 110-115

J

J-bolts, 26, 27
  building stairs, 82
  pouring footings, 58, 61
Jig saw, 31
Joist hangers, 15, 26-27, 40
  hanging joists, 72, 76, 77

Joists, 14-15, 44-45
  decking patterns, 16-17, 99
  double, 16-17, 105, 107
  end, 101
  hanging, 72-77
  header, 14, 46, 48, 51, 74, 101
  outside, 14-15, 74, 101
  plan, 73
  repairing, 122-124
  short, 17
  sister, 122-123
  size and spacing, 25, 73
  span, 25
  trim, 17, 99, 102

K

Knots, lumber, 20-21

L

Lag screws, 26-27
Landings, 18
Lap siding, ledger installation, 46-49
Lattice panels, 10, 19
Laying decking, 79-81
Ledger plan, 53
Ledgers, 14-15, 44
  installation, 46-51, 100
Levels, 30, 34
Line level, 30, 34, 52, 56
Locating post footings, 52-57
Lumber,
  basics, 20-21
  cedar, 14, 20-23, 72, 79, 81
  end grain, 21
  flaws, 21
  heartwood, 20, 23
  ordering, 40-41
  preservatives, 20-23
  pressure-treated, 14, 20-23, 62, 68,
    72, 118-119
  redwood, 14, 20, 22-23, 72, 79,
    81, 99
  sapwood, 20, 23
  size, 24-25
  span, 25
  storage, 21
  types, 22-23
Lumber and materials checklist, 41

M

Maintaining a deck, 120-121
Masonry, ledger installation, 49-50

Masonry anchors, 27, 50
Mason's string, 30
  post footings location, 52, 54-57
  site drawings, 34-35
Materials, ordering, 40-41
Metal cleats, 109
Metal snips, 30
Midwestern deck, 8
Multilevel deck, 6
Multiuse deck, 11

N

Nails, 26, 40

O

Octagonal deck, 110-115
Open steps, 18
Orbital sander, 31, 118
Ordering lumber and materials, 40-41
Outside joists, 14-15, 74, 101, 107, 113
Overview, step-by-step, 44-45

P

Parquet decking pattern, 16
Particle mask, 22, 31
Plan-view drawings, 34-38
Platform deck, 10, 99-103
Platform steps, 18
Plumb bob, 30
  building stairs, 82, 84
  post footings location, 52, 57
  pouring footings, 58, 61
Portland cement, 28-29, 58-61
Post anchors, 14-15, 26-27, 40
  attaching posts, 65-66
  building stairs, 82, 84
  installation, 62-64
Post elevation plan, 64
Post footings, 14, 44-45
  concrete, 28-29
  digging and pouring, 58-61
  location, 52-57, 84
Post plan, 53
Posts, 14-15
  railings, 19
  replacing, 124-125
  setting, 62, 64-67
  size, 24-25

Pouring footings, 58-61
Power augers, digging footings, 58-59
Power drill, 31
Power miter box, 31
Premixed concrete, 28-29
Preshaped products, 19
Pressure sprayer, 31, 118, 120
Pressure-treated deck, finishing, 118-119
Pressure-treated lumber, 20-22
  beams, 14, 68, 69
  finishing, 118-119
  joists, 14, 72
  ledgers, 14, 46-47
  posts, 14, 62
Pruning saw, 58-59
Pry bar, 30, 79-80, 122
Putty knife, 30

R

Railing posts, 14-15, 19
  size and spacing, 25
Railings, 14-15, 19, 45
  horizontal, 19
  installation, 88-95
  plan, 88
  preshaped, 19
  size, 25
Ratchet wrench, 30
Ready-mixed concrete, 28-29
Reciprocating saw, 31
Redwood, 14, 20, 22-23
  facing boards, 79, 81, 99
  header joists, 72
  sealer-preservative, 99
Redwood deck, finishing, 118-119
Renewing a deck, 120-121
Repairing decking and joists, 122-124
Replacing posts, 124-125
Rise, stairs, 82-83
Rubber mallet, 30, 46, 50
Run, stairs, 82-83

S

Sander, orbital, 31
Sapwood, 20, 23
  sealer-preservative, 20, 23, 99
Saws, 31
Scratch awl, 30
Screwgun, 31
Screws, 26, 40
Sealer-preservative, 20-21, 23, 40
  deck finishing, 118-119
  deck repair, 122, 124-125

Sheathing, ledger installation, 46, 48, 51
Silicone caulk, 26, 27, 40
Single-level deck, 8
Sister joists, deck repair, 122-123
Site drawings, 34-35
Span, stairs, 25, 82, 83
Span limits, 24-25
Staining sealers (toners), 118-119
Stair cleats, 27
Stairs, building, 82-87
  span, 82-83
Stairways, 14-15, 18, 45
  measurements, 83
Steps, 18
  boxed, 18
  brackets, 85, 87
  number of, 82, 83
  open, 18
  platform, 18
Stringers, 14-15, 18, 83
  notched, 18, 87
  size, 25
Structural plans, 99, 105, 110
Stucco, ledger installation, 51

T

Toners (staining sealers), 118-119
Tools,
  basics, 31
  beam installation, 68
  building stairs, 82
  deck finishing, 118
  deck maintenance, 120
  deck repair, 122
  design drawings, 36
  digging and pouring footings, 58
  hand, 30-31
  hanging joists, 72
  laying decking, 79
  ledger installation, 46
  post anchor attachment, 62
  post footings location, 52
  power, 31
  railing installation, 88
  setting posts, 62
  site drawings, 34
Torpedo level, 30, 61, 92
Treads, 14-15, 18, 82-83, 86-87
Trim joists, 17
  platform deck, 99
Trowel, 30

U

Utility lines, 44, 58

V

Vacuum, 31, 118, 119
Vertical drop, stairs, 82-83
Vertical rise, 82-83

W

Warm climate deck, 9
Washers, 26

Creative Publishing international, Inc. offers a variety of how-to books.
For information write:
Creative Publishing international, Inc.
Subscriber Books
5900 Green Oak Drive
Minnetonka, MN 55343